Recovering Hegel from the Critique of Leo Strauss

Recovering Hegel from the Critique of Leo Strauss

The Virtues of Modernity

Sara MacDonald and Barry Craig

LEXINGTON BOOKS
Lanham • Boulder • New York • Toronto • Plymouth, UK

Published by Lexington Books
A wholly owned subsidiary of Rowman & Littlefield
4501 Forbes Boulevard, Suite 200, Lanham, Maryland 20706
www.rowman.com

10 Thornbury Road, Plymouth PL6 7PP, United Kingdom

British Library Cataloguing in Publication Information Available

Library of Congress Cataloging-in-Publication Data

MacDonald, Sara (Sara Jane)
Recovering Hegel from the critique of Leo Strauss : the virtues of modernity / Sara MacDonald and Barry Craig.
pages cm.
Includes bibliographical references.
ISBN 978-0-7391-8397-7 (cloth : alk. paper)—ISBN 978-0-7391-8398-4 (ebook)
1. Hegel, Georg Wilhelm Friedrich, 1770–1831. 2. Strauss, Leo. 3. Civilization, Modern. I. Title.
B2948.M136 2014
193—dc23
2013034366

∞™ The paper used in this publication meets the minimum requirements of American National Standard for Information Sciences Permanence of Paper for Printed Library Materials, ANSI/NISO Z39.48-1992.

Printed in the United States of America

To Patrick, Mary, and Catherine

Contents

Preface

We have both been fortunate to have good teachers throughout our respective educations. To one of us, while an undergraduate student at St. Thomas University, political philosophy was introduced by Professors Rick Myers and Patrick Malcolmson. This introduction, which included the first reading of Leo Strauss, was deepened during graduate study at Fordham, through the guidance and help of Mary Nichols, Michael and Catherine Zuckert, and Michael Davis. While both scholars are generally counted as "Straussians," the breadth of their thought, as well as their intellectual generosity, encouraged students to look beyond any narrow ideological approach. Thus, it was there also that Hegel became an object of study. To the other of us, Leo Strauss was introduced via the many hours spent in and out of class with the Canadian political philosopher George Grant, an ardent admirer of Strauss's work and equally ardent critic of Hegel. Hegel was introduced by Grant's colleagues Wayne Hankey and James Doull, the latter a relatively unknown Canadian thinker, who was nevertheless once described by Emil Fackenheim as "the only Hegelian." Now, from a distance of some thirty years, the depth and rigor of their scholarship is even more impressive. Since our initial respective exposures to Strauss and Hegel, a couple of decades of intellectual ferment, and countless conversations over glasses of wine, have led to this present work.

While the ancient world has its attractions, and indeed, in our view, though the thought of Aristotle, and especially Plato, remains the source of understanding out of which all subsequent western thought has grown, and without which none of subsequent western thought can be truly comprehended, we cannot accept the ancient social order in which such thought was born. Leo Strauss was initially attractive to us, as he has been to countless others, because he was unafraid to cast a critical eye on many of the intellectual sacred cows of modernity. His radical reappropriation of ancient thought and his idiosyncratic readings of the history of philosophy caused us to challenge our own preconceptions and unexamined assumptions about the world in which we live. Questioning whether or not democracy was simply good, or whether freedom and equality were, by themselves, adequate conditions for human flourishing was both challenging and exhilarating at the same time. In Strauss the challenge of historicism and its effects on the possibility of knowledge or truth was presented in a clear and provocative manner.

And yet, we both had long harbored an unsettling apprehension that this conservative critique of modernity, while justified in many particulars, was incomplete, if not simply wrong, in some fundamental way. The progress of women's right alone, let alone the abolition of slavery and the recognition of other fundamental and universal human rights seemed to us such undoubted goods and so clearly products specifically of modernity that we could not ultimately remain satisfied with Strauss's account. Thus, about a decade ago, we began putting together the argument of this book. While one of our teachers, Robert Crouse, once wisely cautioned against enshrining any one philosopher as possessing the absolute truth, we nevertheless believe that Hegel had a more complete account of the end and purpose of human life than any thinker before or since. That is because Hegel labored to produce a philosophic system that included both the objective and absolute together with the subjective elements of reality. Despite the many limitations of Hegel's thought, some caused by the particularities of his own historical epoch or the incompleteness of his historical and cultural scholarship, he offered the best opportunity for uniting what was good about the thought of Greek antiquity (i.e., an account of transcendent truth and human virtue) with what was best about the spirit of modernity (i.e., human freedom and individual subjectivity).

The history of Hegelian scholarship, as is well known, is a tale of disagreement and division. For the most part, and this began immediately upon Hegel's death, the camps of interpretation have been divided between the Left and the Right of the political spectrum. Uncomfortable with the absolute forms of either ideology, we instead found in Hegel a middle ground (we are far from the first to discover this) which offered a way out of the polarization of political thought, and indeed, contemporary culture wars. This reading, which owed much to the thought and writings of James Doull, recovered the objective side of Hegel's thought while insisting on the value of his insistence on subjective freedom. That he took seriously Hegel's religious thought perhaps offers a partial explanation of why Doull's own work was not embraced in the mainstream of contemporary western philosophy. Rather than opposing duty and rights, law and freedom, or objective truth and subjective feeling, Doull demonstrated that Hegel's thought brought together those opposed sides as not only compatible but necessary elements of the whole. From this, it is possible for a conservative who values the thought of Plato and his account of the Good to see the necessity of freedom and individual self-consciousness if this idea is to be manifest in the world.

As is clear from the many references in the text to the work of others, we recognize that elements of this argument have been advanced by other scholars, both within and outside of the Straussian school and across various strands of the Hegelian schools. Hopefully, in this book we have succeeded in gathering up many of these elements and presenting them them in a way that is at once accurate and fair as well as clear and accessible both to non-specialist readers and to students of political philosophy who have an interest in the thought of both Hegel and Strauss. In our efforts towards clarity and accessibility, we have necessarily resisted engaging in depth many of the technical aspects of Hegelian thought. Given the widely divergent interpretations that surround both thinkers, we are cognizant that some of the interpretations we have advanced, of both Hegel and Strauss, and some of the conclusions we have drawn with respect to contemporary social and political developments, will not go without criticism. However, at the very least, it is our hope that we have offered something new to the conversation and have enabled a reconsideration of one element of contemporary political philosophy.

In addition to the debt of gratitude we owe to our own teachers, mentioned above, over the decade that we have been discussing and then writing this book, we have been helped by many people, not least many of our students, who have assisted with research, proofreading, and the kinds of arguments that inspire us to think more deeply and engage our own presuppositions from fresh angles. Among these many students, we owe particular thanks to Mark Adams, Ted Jones, Matt Dinan, Vivien Zelazny, Nathan McAllister, Ruthie Luff, Chelsea Ogilvie, Lacey Texamo, and Amanda Jardine. We have been supported throughout this process by our own institution, St. Thomas University, which has supplied us with time and funding to allow us to pursue our research. Finally, we wish to thank Patrick, Mary, and Catherine who, over the time we have been preparing and then writing this book, have moved from being children to teenagers and then young adults. They were at times sources of inspiration, or at least distraction, when it was most helpful. As many have learned before us, Hegel's complexity can becoming all consuming, and regular reminders of the "real world" recall us to why we were attracted to the love of wisdom in the first place. To us, philosophy is not merely abstract or analytical in nature, but the means to understand the most profound truths of the human condition. This understanding can then inform the impulse to contribute to a more just and charitable society.

Introduction

In recent years much attention, both scholarly and popular, has been paid to the work of Leo Strauss. Born in 1899 in Hesse, Germany, to an observant Jewish family, Strauss completed a PhD at University of Hamburg (1921). His subsequent studies and work in philosophy and political philosophy brought him into contact with Edmund Husserl, Martin Heidegger, Hans-Georg Gadamer, and, as we shall see, Alexander Kojève. Strauss's contributions to the field of political philosophy have been significant in terms of the strength and diversity of his publications ranging across ancient, medieval, and modern political philosophy. A strong following of devoted students continue in his footsteps and his influence on contemporary American political philosophy has been profound.

This influence has also been the basis for significant attacks against Strauss both in terms of his methodology and his perceived political influence. Most recently Strauss has been condemned as the intellectual father of the neoconservative movement and the political reign of George W. Bush. Many of the attacks against Strauss and his students have been extreme and personal in nature. For example, one of Strauss's most vocal critics, Shadia Drury, has gone so far as to declare, "The trouble with the Straussians is that they are compulsive liars."[1] Allegations such as these have resulted in several strong defenses of Strauss as a thinker and mentor.[2] It is not the purpose of this book to enter into that fray. We are neither students of American politics nor close enough to the inner circle of Straussians to be able to adequately comment on either. Nonetheless, we do believe that many of the attacks against Strauss's work are unfounded, and we have been fortunate to learn a great deal from his close analyses of many of the West's most influential philosophic texts as well as from the many works of his students and associates.

Our argument, however, is not wholly disconnected from the recent debate, nor is it uncritical of Strauss. One of the many judgments levied against Strauss and his followers is that their reading of the history of philosophy encourages a conservative political agenda that is elitist and tyrannical. We believe that these claims are overstated. Yet it is clear that Strauss was critical of particular trends in modernity, specifically, its emphasis on individual subjectivity and unlimited freedom. The philosophy of G.W.F. Hegel, Strauss suggests, contributed significantly to the wrongful path of modernity. Virtue, Strauss argues, should take precedence over freedom in one's private and political life. Modern people ought to look to antiquity, he argues, as it provides an alternative and perhaps even better model of the highest human life.

At the same time that interest in Leo Strauss has increased, there has been an unrelated renewed interest in the philosophy of Hegel. While some conservatives look to Strauss as perhaps a means to salvage the modern world from its ills, other scholars have re-engaged Hegel's thought to determine if it might yet have any relevance to the contemporary order.[3] While Strauss viewed Hegel's thought as indicative of much that is wrong with liberalism and modernity, for many contemporary thinkers, Hegel's position is not liberal enough. Hegel's emphasis on an objective rational principle, the nature and power of the state, his particular treatment of the inequality of men and women, and the necessity of war, all seem to suggest that Hegel's thought is the by-product of a now rightly forgotten earlier age.

Yet neither Strauss's conservative criticisms nor those stemming from more liberal thinkers are fair to the fullness of Hegel's project. Siding fully with neither the right nor the left, Hegel seeks to show that the principles of each side can only be fulfilled when they are reconciled with what seems to be their opposite part. Wisdom and virtue, on the one hand, and freedom and diversity, on the other, are mutually dependent.

This book examines Strauss's critique of modernity in light of Hegel's philosophic defense of the same. In so doing, we hope to reveal that many of the virtues of the ancient world that Strauss and other conservatives have feared as lost can only properly be present when individual particularity and subjectivity are recognized and fulfilled. Despite the strength of Strauss's critique, we will argue that Hegel's thought regarding the nature of modernity addresses and even satisfies many, if not all, of Strauss's concerns. In the process we will necessarily shed light on the other side of the debate. For those who would stress Hegel's conservatism, rightly attending to Strauss's criticisms of Hegel brings to the light the essentially liberal nature of Hegel's thought. In the end, we agree with Hegel: virtue and freedom are not opposed, but each is necessary for the other. In the following chapters we will delve into the similarities and differences of the philosophic accounts of Strauss and Hegel. For the purposes of an introduction, however, we will briefly state the position of each, setting the stage for the debate that will follow.

THE ANCIENT QUEST FOR WISDOM AND VIRTUE

In determining the best life for a human being, Strauss narrows the possibilities to two: the philosophic life and the life of ethical virtue, as exemplified, Strauss says, in the life of the gentleman. Largely in agreement with Aristotle's argument in the *Nicomachean Ethics*, Strauss suggests that the highest human life will be one that most appropriately uses the best part of our natures.[4] Insofar as reason is judged as being what most distinctively marks a human being in relationship to other natural beings, the best human life will be one that most appropriately makes use of our rational faculty, seeking to understand the truest of things. Initially, it seems that Strauss judges the life of wisdom as the best human life. Focused on what is eternally true, the wise person's happiness would be most stable and he would be most content. However, Strauss also notes that what is actually best must not exist only hypothetically, but in reality. In this light, a life of wisdom cannot be the best life, for, as we shall see, Strauss argues that the absolute is ultimately inscrutable to a human intellect. As such, Strauss judges the achievement of human wisdom as impossible. Nonetheless, he argues, one might seek to know, and in seeking one might gain some understanding and some relative degree of happiness. Socrates may only know that he knows nothing, but at least he knows that.

The idea that the life of the philosopher might be the best possible life is complicated when we recognize that the insufficiency of human nature makes life in a community necessary. People are not just rational beings; they are rational animals, and the animalistic side of human existence, i.e., the body, requires a great deal of care. The time and effort it takes to simply remain alive is time and effort that cannot be spent in contemplation. Life in a community alleviates some of this stress, but also adds difficulties of its own. Now, in addition to attending to the health of their bodies, individuals must also think about the health of their communities, if only for the sake of their continued well-being.

In recognizing the need for communities, Strauss argues a potentially second-best life emerges—the life of the *kaloi kagathoi*, those who are beautiful and good, the gentlemen. In the gentleman, Strauss argues that ethical activity rather than contemplation is prominent. The gentleman uses reason to govern himself, particularly his appetitive self, and seeks to assist in governing others through active participation in his city. Given the necessity of living in community, and the emphasis that the gentleman places on rational activity, the public life of a gentleman, or statesman, competes with the happiness of the philosopher.

Ultimately, Strauss sides with the philosopher. While the philosopher will never reach the truth and, hence, will always be unsatisfied, a gentleman has to serve the city he governs and he depends on the city—a thing that is divided and mutable—for his happiness. Such a person leads a life "of perpetual business, care and trouble."[5] The philosopher, alternatively, serves and depends on no one, other than the truth, and is as free as is humanly possible.[6] While the circumstances of a city and the affections of people change and cannot be counted on, the truth, while impossible to fully grasp, always remains the same. The philosopher, aware of his progress on the path to truth, can derive pleasure, satisfaction, and happiness from the knowledge that he is closer to the end he seeks than he was before.[7] The political life cannot afford this level of certainty.

There is the additional question of the relative virtue possible within these lives, for "true happiness . . . is possible only on the basis of excellence."[8] Political virtue, Strauss says, is qualified. A gentleman is virtuous, at least in part, because he seeks to be honored, if not by everyone, then at least by those capable of doing so.[9] We are to understand that true virtue lies in doing what one ought to do, regardless of the consequences, and regardless of whether one's virtuous deeds are recognized. Insofar as he seeks to be honored for his virtue, the gentleman is not virtuous in the fullest sense. The philosopher, however, seeks the good, in and of itself, regardless of whether his achievement is recognized by others. The true philosopher seeks wisdom for its own sake.

Finally, Strauss concludes that the relative dependence of the gentleman, in contrast with the independence of the philosopher, means that the philosopher is more likely to act properly in his relationships with others. Strauss writes, "Since the wise man does not need human beings in the way in which, and to the extent to which, the ruler does, his attitude toward them is free, not passionate, and hence not susceptible of turning into malevolence or hatred . . . the wise man alone is capable of justice in the highest sense."[10] While we might object that the philosopher, who seems to care for nothing other than the truth, seems cold, Strauss suggests that this coldness is a virtue. The philosopher will be moved by neither sentiment nor petty desire when dealing with others. The gentleman, alternatively, is tied to the city so that no matter how he might seek to govern his desires, there is the chance that his motivation will be less than objective.

In the contest between the gentleman, or statesman, and the philosopher, Strauss declares the philosopher the clear victor. Yet, he also concedes that the life of the gentleman is a more likely option for more people and a close second with respect to relative virtue and satisfaction. Moreover, Strauss understands that the habituation of the gentleman to virtue and the common good makes him open to the possibility of philosophy. However and crucially, Strauss also notes neither the life of the true philosopher nor that of the gentleman is encouraged within modernity. Instead, by accepting the main tenets of historicism, modern philosophy has jettisoned even the idea of an objective truth. All truth is now subjective and so all people can now be "philosophers."[11] Correspondingly, the political world's endorsement of freedom as at the heart of human nature and, therefore, at the heart of justice, means that all activities, with the exception of those that might infringe on other freedoms, are equally valued. All people might thus be "gentlemen." Needless to say, for Strauss, these modern philosophers and gentlemen fall far short of the original and true form of these lives properly understood.

MODERN FREEDOM

Hegel, alternatively, sees modernity as having progressed beyond the position of the ancient world. Recognizing the truth inherent in ancient philosophy, Hegel understands the place of virtue and philosophy in the best human life. Nonetheless, Hegel says that antiquity erred in preferring only the objective and universal element in human nature to the detriment of human nature as it particularly and subjectively exists. While a few people, perhaps, could be satisfied in knowing that they have done or sought the good regardless of the demands of their more particular desires, most people, Hegel understands, could not. Instead, faced with objective demands that they act in accordance with what is objectively best, even if that means sacrificing all of their own particular aims and interests, the majority of people will find other means, often subversive, to satisfy their desires.

Even further, Hegel writes that disregarding subjectivity as a necessary and even positive part of human consciousness, the ancient order failed to understand human nature and the best human life. Hegel agrees with the ancients that the capacity for thought and rational activity are fundamentally part of what it means to be human. Yet to recognize the complexity of a human life, all elements of the human nature must be fully accounted for.

Modernity, Hegel argues, advances beyond the limited vision of antiquity by appreciating the role of individual subjectivity. Politically, this understanding is expressed in the promulgation of laws that protect human rights. Recognizing that individuals are diverse, liberal democratic regimes presuppose that justice requires the free expression of these differences. Such regimes understand that people will choose different paths based on their particular talents and interests, and that most, if not all, of these choices will be appropriate and rational despite, and even because of, the differences that inspire them. In so doing, these political communities signal that they recognize the capacity of individuals to make rational choices with their freedom.

While Strauss argues that modernity has gone too far in promoting subjectivity over and against the recognition of any objective good, Hegel disagrees. Instead, Hegel argues that modernity allows for the possibility of a fully actualized ethical life, a possibility, he says, that is not present in antiquity. Unlike the ethical life of antiquity where unreflective custom dominates, in modern ethical life, or *sittlichkeit*, Hegel, according to Allen Wood, describes "a rational institutional structure, whose rationality makes it desirable by individuals as an end in itself, and not merely as a means to individual good."[12] Ethical life combines the particular tastes, desires, and talents of individuals with an objectively true and good order. By recognizing, protecting, and incorporating individual choices and preferences, modern political communities encourage individuals to recognize the goodness of these communities and support them. This, Hegel suggests, is more than "enlightened self-interest," where one concedes the existence of the larger whole because it is of some benefit to oneself. Instead, Hegel argues that, in a modern ethical state, individual preferences and desires are transformed or broadened such that these individuals take up what is good for the whole alongside what might be good for themselves.

In a liberal democratic regime, individuals perceive their true nature as manifested in the objective institutions and laws of their political communities. In their protected rights, they see the inherent truth of their subjective and particular lives. At the same time, they understand that they can be trusted with the execution of these particular preferences not because these choices are unimportant, but rather because these individuals are also rational, thinking beings. The onus is on them to reasonably execute their preferences. Seeing themselves in the objective order of their political communities, and finding themselves inherently satisfied therein, these individuals should also recognize the rationality and goodness of their political orders and begin to see its ends as consistent with their own. Rather than leading to a state of decadence and corruption, Hegel believes that modernity can be the source of virtue and happiness.

Although Strauss seems primarily pessimistic about the modern project, there are aspects of his understanding of the best life that seem more closely aligned with modernity than he publicly states. Moreover, Strauss is not entirely negative with respect to Hegel's thought, referring to Hegel in one instance as "the outstanding philosopher of the nineteenth century."[13] And also noting that: "Hegel returned from the philosophy of reflection to the higher vitality of Plato and Aristotle."[14] This has led some commentators to suggest that although subtle about his agreement with many modern things, Strauss was not a proponent of the ancient world over and against the modern.[15] We do not want to make that argument; instead, we will take Strauss's position at face value. According to Strauss, ancient political thought and the world that it created are preferred to the modern equivalent. If this is an accurate assessment of Strauss's thought, we believe it relies on a false dichotomy—that political freedom and virtue are irreconcilable. In contrast, Hegel's view of modernity provides a more optimistic and, indeed, truer picture. For, Hegel agrees fundamentally with Strauss's interpretation of the main tenets of ancient philosophy and, in addition, provides a foundation for the philosophic freedom that Strauss agrees is the best possible option. Yet this is a resolution that Strauss denies or avoids.

CHAPTER OUTLINE

While we believe that Strauss and Hegel agree on many significant points, we also think that Hegel's philosophy and the modern world offer a superior vision of human ends and human community than either that of antiquity or the vision presented by Strauss. Strauss may have endorsed liberal democratic regimes as being the best possible political communities; yet, philosophically, he preferred ancient thought and inevitably this kind of conservatism makes its way, intentionally or not, into the political force of his writing. Even within Strauss's essays it is relatively easy to see a conservative political pattern emerge and it is perhaps not unfair to draw this to the forefront given that Strauss believed and argued that philosophy shapes the basis of our political and moral existences.

For example, in a letter to Karl Löwith, a young Strauss writes, "Just because . . . right-wing Germany does not tolerate us [the Jews] says nothing against the principles of the right. To the contrary, only on the basis of the principles of the right—fascist, authoritarian, imperial—is it possible, with decency and without the ridiculous and pitiable appeal to the 'unwritten rights of man,' to protest against this shabby nuisance [i.e., Hitler]."[16] While Strauss's position seems to have moderated through the course of the war and his life in America, Steven Smith observes, "This letter has been widely discussed . . . as evidence of a strong authoritarian streak in Strauss's thought. This judgment may not be altogether false."[17] In an essay on the crisis facing modernity, Strauss favorably describes a similarity between the classical view and a faithful observance of the Bible, writing that each agrees "that the proper framework of morality is the patriarchal family, which is, or tends to be, monogamous, and which forms the cell of society in which free adult males, and especially the old ones, predominate."[18] The politically conservative conclusions that one might draw from such a statement are obvious. It is then not surprising that students or followers of Strauss have often been identified as associated with conservative political agendas.[19]

In disagreement with Strauss, we will argue that Hegel's philosophy offers an approach to liberal democratic politics that is in fact more conducive to the happiness and virtue of its citizens than that envisioned by either the ancients or by Strauss. Recognizing the true particularity of human nature, the Hegelian political order includes human beings in all of their natural diversity. In so doing, it encourages and endorses their rational participation within the whole. We believe that Strauss either misconstrued or disagreed with Hegel's project on several important, and connected, grounds. The following chapters will examine Strauss's position, and try to give as clear a response as possible in light of Hegel's argument.

Although seemingly critical of Hegelian thought, it is Hegel's thought as read through the lens of Alexander Kojève that Strauss finds most disquieting. In chapter 1 we will outline Kojève's understanding of Hegel as well as his vision of the nature of modernity. Although Kojève, like Hegel, is a proponent of modernity, the account he has of the modern world differs dramatically from what Hegel understood. With this perspective of modernity accounted for, we will explore the elements of this argument that Strauss disagrees with before we turn our attention in the later chapters to how Hegel might have potentially responded. In brief, Strauss argues that this account of Hegel's philosophy unleashes human desire and ultimately results in an empire, the very nature of which will be either tyrannical or altogether unsatisfactory for human existence. As a result, Strauss is able to see even the nihilism of Nietzsche as a welcome break from Hegelian mediocrity.

While Strauss's particular critique of Hegel's account of modernity is generally acknowledged in scholarship, in the second chapter we will argue that the roots of Strauss's divergence from Hegel's thought lie in metaphysics rather than in politics or ethics. In our interpretation of Hegel's metaphysical foundations, we are in agreement with Wood who argues:

> it is not as though Hegel's social philosophy drives us back to the categories of metaphysics as to some source of esoteric wisdom. The point is rather that Hegel sees his metaphysics as the foundation of a philosophy that deals with the modern predicament because his own deepest response to the modern predicament is a response on the level of metaphysics . . . Hegel seeks to overcome alienation by rationally reconciling us to the world, comprehending a divine reason, akin to our own, immanent in it.[20]

The primary difficulty with Strauss's understanding of Hegel is that Strauss believes that Hegel envisions a wholly secular world, or a world where there is no recognized relationship to, or dependence on, a universal metaphysical principle. It is our contention that Strauss's unwillingness to accept, or at least acknowledge, Hegel's claims about Christianity and Christian philosophy largely account for Strauss's misunderstanding of Hegel. While Strauss accepts Kojève's presentation of Hegel's "religious" position, Strauss's own tendency to radically separate religion and philosophy is what makes him susceptible to Kojève's arguments.

Next, as will be discussed in the third and fourth chapters, we address what is perhaps the most significant criticism lodged against Hegel: that the perfect ethical order he argues in favor of has not yet come into existence. Even if we reject Kojève's argument necessitating the world homogenous state, do we not have to admit that the modern order is not all that ethical? In partial agreement with this critique, we argue that the contemporary world represents, in large part, the penultimate stage of morality that Hegel describes as preceding the state of ethical life. We have not yet achieved, in any complete way, the highest stage of ethical life that Hegel depicts. However, as we will argue in the fourth chapter, there are indicators in the modern world that show we are progressing to a more ethical state, one that is closely aligned with Hegel's vision.

Strauss's thought has gained considerable negative attention in recent years, and while many of the criticisms against his arguments are ultimately unfounded, it is possible to discern the source of these concerns. The conservative nature of Strauss's thought and the seemingly unbridgeable gap between the politics of the far right and far left leaves many of the clerics in this debate preaching only to choirs of the converted. We think that Hegel's thought, if attended to, could serve to reconcile some of these estrangements, or at least assist in ensuring that the separation is amiable. Hegel is an unqualified supporter of modernity and the messiness this entails. At the same time, he believes that it is this world that will bring to fruition many of the most important aspirations of the ancients. Freedom, virtue, and philosophy, Hegel argues, are inseparable and one who would practically limit the first will necessarily concede the loss of the other two. Neither Hegel nor Strauss imagines that all people will use their freedom well and become virtuous and thus philosophic. Instead, Hegel argues that the contemporary world confirms that people will be drawn to lives of greater decency and enlightenment if given greater practical freedom, an idea with which we agree. One might charge that this is a naïve or nearsighted thought. As Hegel, however, tells us, "reason is the rose in the cross of the present."[21] Despite, and even because of, the weaknesses associated with the inevitable imperfections and tremendous failings of any world at any time, we are given a way to see what is true and our path forward.

AUDIENCE

This book is primarily aimed at scholars in political science or political philosophy who have an interest in the work and influence of Leo Strauss, those who are concerned that the modern world may not be as conducive to virtue or true human happiness as previous eras, as well as those who are interested in defending the modern world. Given the possibility that not everyone in our target audience will be as familiar with Hegel's writing, we have tried to explicate our understanding of Hegel's argument in as clear and jargon-free a manner as possible. While we have sought to clearly indicate where we stand in the recent scholarly debates concerning Hegelian interpretation, we have tried not to get bogged down in the minutiae of these debates. Instead, we indicate the various sides of the debates in question, explain our position, and then move forward. Additionally, scholars of Hegel should find our application of Hegelian thought to contemporary issues to be of interest.

NOTES

1. Shadia Drury, "Saving America," Evatt Foundation, last modified September, 2003, http://evatt.org.au/papers/saving-america.html.

2. Further critiques of Strauss include, William H. F. Altman, *The German Stranger: Leo Strauss and National Socialism* (Maryland: Lexington Books, 2010); Shadia Drury, *Leo Strauss and the American Right* (London: Palgrave Macmillan, 1999); Ann Norton, *Leo Strauss and the Politics of American Empire* (New Haven: Yale University Press, 2004); and Earl Shorris, "Ignoble Liars: Leo Strauss, George Bush, and the Philosophy of Mass Deception," *Harper's Magazine*, June 2004, 308:1849, 65–71. Defenses or reconsiderations of Strauss's thought include Peter Minowitz, *Straussophobia: Defending Leo Strauss and Straussians against Shadia Drury and Other Accusers* (Lanham: Lexington Books, 2009); Thomas Pangle, *Leo Strauss: An Introduction to His Thought and Intellectual Legacy* (Baltimore: John Hopkins University Press, 2006); and Catherine and Michael Zuckert, *The Truth about Leo Strauss* (Chicago: University of Chicago Press, 2006).

3. For instance, in the past five years alone, the following is a selection of only a few of the scholarly books that have been written on the question of Hegel's continued relevance, Andrew Buchwalter, *Dialectics, Politics, and the Contemporary Value of Hegel's Practical Philosophy* (New York: Routledge, 2012); Katerinia Deligiorgi, *Hegel New Directions* (Chesham, Bucks: Acumen, 2006); Thomas Lewis, *Religion, Modernity, and Politics in Hegel* (New York: Oxford University Press, 2011); Lydia Moland, *Hegel on Political Identity: Patriotism, Nationality, Cosmopolitanism* (Chicago: Northwestern University Press, 2011); Frederick Neuhouser, *Foundations of Hegel's Social Theory* (Cambridge: Harvard University Press, 2000); Robert C. Sibley, *Northern Spirits: John Watson, George Grant, and Charles Taylor: Appropriations of Hegelian Political Thought* (Montreal: McGill Queen's University Press, 2012); Slavoj Žižek, Clayton Crockett, and Creston Davis, *Hegel & the Infinite: Religion, politics, and dialectic* (New York: Columbia Press, 2012).

4. Aristotle, *Nicomachean Ethics*, trans. Terence Irwin (Indianapolis: Hackett Publishing, Co., 2000), 1177a, 15–20.

5. Leo Strauss, "On Tyranny," in *On Tyranny* (New York: Free Press, 1991), 84.

6. Ibid., 84 and 91.

7. Ibid., 101.

8. Ibid., 82.

9. Ibid., 101.

10. Ibid., 91. See also 99.

11. Leo Strauss, "On Aristotle's Politics," in *The City and Man* (Chicago: Rand McNally, 1964), 37.

12. Allen W. Wood, *Hegel's Ethical Thought* (Cambridge: Cambridge University Press, 1990), 1999.

13. Leo Strauss, "Political Philosophy and History," in *What is Political Philosophy? and Other Studies* (Glencoe: The Free Press, 1958), p. 58.

14. Leo Strauss, "What is Political Philosophy," in *What is Political Philosophy*, 51.

15. Victor Gourevitch, "Philosophy and Politics, I," *The Review of Metaphysics* 22 (1968): 58–84; 281–328. For an interesting account of the Strauss's thought in relationship to the American regime, see Zuckert, "The Truth about Leo Strauss."

16. As quoted in Steven Smith, "Leo Strauss: The Outline of a Life," in *The Cambridge Companion to Leo Strauss* (Cambridge: Cambridge University Press, 2009), 19.

17. Smith, "Leo Strauss: The Outline of a Life," 19–21.

18. Leo Strauss, "Progress or Return," in *The Rebirth of Classical Political Rationalism* (Indianapolis: University of Chicago Press, 1989), 247.

19. For instance, see Drury, *The Political Ideas of Leo Strauss*, and Norton, *Leo Strauss and the Politics of American Empire*.
20. Allen W. Wood, *Hegel's Ethical Thought* (Cambridge: Cambridge University Press, 1990), 6–7.
21. G.W.F. Hegel, *Elements of the Philosophy of Right*, trans. H.B. Nisbet (Cambridge: Cambridge University Press, 1991), Preface 22.

ONE

Strauss's Critique of Modernity

Strauss does not write at length directly about Hegel's philosophy. However, in responding to the thought of Alexander Kojève, noted left-wing Hegelian scholar, proponent of modernity, and Strauss's friend, Strauss provides a focal point for his understanding of Hegel and his critique of the modern world. Strauss and Kojève met while both were students in Berlin. Although Kojève settled in France until his death in 1968, he and Strauss continued their friendship through correspondence until at least 1965. Their written communication is collected in *On Tyranny*, a collaborative work between the two that is noted as marking the beginning of Strauss's scholarly focus on the debate between the ancients and moderns.[1]

Ultimately, we will argue that had Strauss moved more fully through Kojève's interpretation of Hegel to the philosophy of Hegel himself, he would have been confronted with a much stronger account of the possibilities of a philosophical and ethical modern world. Interestingly, while Strauss does not write at length about Hegel, he taught seminars devoted to Hegel's thought, focusing primarily on *The Philosophy of History*, but also *The Logic* and *The Phenomenology*. At least two of these courses were recorded. In attending to these lectures, one realizes that Strauss's understanding of Hegel is, at the very least, more nuanced than what he projects in his published writing. However, unlike Hegel's published lecture notes, which, for better or worse, have been significantly edited by his students and by later scholars, Strauss's lectures are more free-flowing. The classes in questions are seminars and in his comments Strauss appears at times to be responding to seminar papers to which we do not have access. Correspondingly, his classes are quite interactive, and his train of thought is often interrupted by students' questions, many of which are inaudible on the tapes. While Strauss's graciousness in his lengthy responses to his students must have been appreciated, it sometimes means that his lectures are disjointed. The nature of the technology of the age also meant that the audiotapes would have to be changed usually mid-class, meaning that some of what Strauss was saying has been lost in those gaps. Access to these lectures has greatly enhanced our understanding of Strauss's position; however, the above difficulties make it problematic to rely too heavily on these lectures alone. We have instead focused our attention primarily on Strauss's published works. However, in instances when Strauss's lecture comments demonstrate an important divergence, or more complicated understanding of Hegel than his published record, we have sought to note the difference in the text.

Importantly, in the 1958 version of Strauss's Seminar in Political Philosophy: Hegel's *Philosophy of History*, Strauss says that Kojève's *Introduction to the Study of Hegel* is "one of the most valuable [books] on Hegel of which [he] knows."[2] Kojève is a strong advocate for a particular understanding of modernity, one that he suggests is derived from a close reading of Hegel's philosophy, particularly, *The Phenomenology of Spirit*. As Strauss's critique of the modern world was strongly influenced by Kojève's understanding, this is where we will begin as well.

ON TYRANNY

The book that eventually became *On Tyranny* began as Strauss's translation of and commentary on Xenophon's dialogue *Hiero or Tyrannicus*, which Strauss asked Kojève to review.[3] Kojève then proposed that the translation, commentary, Kojève's response, and subsequent rejoinder from Strauss be published as a book.[4] The resulting volume, which can now be found with their letters to one another appended, is remarkable in both form and content.

Strauss writes *On Tyranny* with the explicit intent to portray and critique modern political life and provide, in contrast, an ancient alternative. He invites Kojève to write what he knows will be a strong, if particular, defense of the modern world, which Strauss then answers.[5] Kojève's interpretation of Hegel's thought, although a poor account of Hegel, is excellent at synthesizing and distilling the modern philosophic tradition that Strauss finds so problematic. Strauss is aware that this reading of Hegel is idiosyncratic. The expanded version of *On Tyranny*, including Strauss's response to Kojève, was published in French in 1948, in English in 1954, and then again revised in English in 1963. The existing lectures we have from Strauss are from 1958 and 1965, with natural differences in emphasis and explanation, but in each he presents fundamentally the same account of Hegel. As stated above, the account we get of Hegel in the lectures shows a more complicated and nuanced version than that presented in Strauss's discussion of *Hiero*. Nonetheless, even in the last revised version of *On Tyranny* Strauss allows Kojève to be the mouthpiece for Hegelianism because it is this account of modernity that Strauss finds so troubling. *On Tyranny* deliberately sets the ancient and modern positions side by side, and although Strauss gets the final word, we have the sense that, as readers, we need only examine the arguments as presented and determine which is superior.

In its opening pages, Strauss writes that the modern world, and modern social science in particular, cannot recognize tyranny despite the presence of the most explicitly tyrannical regimes.[6] Having relinquished the quest for any objective truth, outside of the realm of empirical evidence, questions of the relative goodness or badness of a regime are no longer possible. Value judgments are as inappropriate as they are unscientific, leaving the modern world in a position whereby it can no longer condemn bad rulers or bad states. This reality renders the subjects of such regimes vulnerable, and without any external political or moral support.

Strauss is not ultimately hopeful about the prospect of eradicating tyranny from the political landscape, suggesting instead that it is an interminable problem of human nature.[7] Still, he argues one should seek to understand the nature and causes of tyranny so as to try to avoid its most debilitating effects.[8] Strauss believes ancient political thought, particularly that of Xenophon's *Hiero*, is the clearest window for a modern individual to the nature of tyranny. In *Hiero*, as Strauss presents it, Xenophon takes up the modern or Machiavellian position on tyranny, but with the clear eyes and judgment of an ancient writer.[9]

Hiero consists of a conversation between the tyrant, Hiero, and the poet and possibly wise man, Simonides. Hiero, we learn, is so unhappy that killing himself seems like the only solution. In search of love, Hiero turns to his citizens who display more fear and hatred than love. Fortunately, Simonides has a fix. All Hiero has to do is become a beneficent ruler, one who looks to the well-being of his citizens, thinking of them as comrades rather than as potential threats and enemies. As a result, Simonides claims that Hiero might gain the love of his subjects and the whole world. The ostensible topic of Hiero's and Simonides's conversation revolves around what life is to be preferred, that of the private person or that of the tyrant. However, to say that the book is about the desirability of tyranny, whether ancient or modern, is misleading. While *Hiero* is explicitly about whether the life of a tyrant or private person is best, Strauss, through his commentary and "Restatement," indicates that all forms of political life are in some fashion tyrannical.[10] As such, the real question of *On Tyranny* is whether the life of politics or the life of philosophy is the best life, with the suggestion that the ancients chose the latter while the modern world chooses the former.

Even this, however, is not really (or not only) what is at stake in *On Tyranny*. For in framing the question in this fashion, one assumes that a philosophic and political life are incommensurable, thereby presuming that the nature of wisdom and truth is such that it is ultimately incompatible or unattainable for a human being whose nature dictates life in a *polis*. As such, *On Tyranny* is about the essence of human beings and the truth itself. Strauss believes that our understanding of these things is at the root of the debate between ancients and moderns.

The fullness of truth, according to Strauss, is ultimately beyond the realm of human thought. As infinite and eternal, truth is seen as incompatible with the limitations of a finite human mind. The only option for a human being who seeks the happiest possible life is to live as isolated as possible from the multiple distractions of his finite existence, for the sake of focusing as closely as possible on the Absolute itself. It is in response to Strauss's interpretation of *Hiero* that Kojève most clearly delineates the modern possibility that he understands to be the basis of human satisfaction.

Contrary to those who, like Strauss, argue that there is an unbridgeable divide between the infinite nature of truth and the finite nature of human beings, Kojève argues that the truth makes itself manifest in and through time by means of human activity. The truth is not external to human life, but rather exists and is revealed only by means of human thought and action: "If Being creates itself ("becomes") in the course of History, then it is not in isolating oneself from History that one can reveal Being. . . . In order to reveal Being, the philosopher must . . . participate in history, and it is not clear why he should not then participate in it *actively*."[11] Kojève's argument that the truth is made manifest in human history means that there is no necessary divide between the life of the philosopher, or the best life, and that of the politically active person, or even, as Kojève notes, the tyrant. Instead, it is only by means of political activity that the philosopher is motivated to seek the truth and ultimately confirm the correctness of what he understands. We shall see this argument worked out in more detail shortly through Kojève's *Introduction to the Reading of Hegel*. Although Kojève's argument in this respect bears some similarity to that of Hegel and, indeed, he claims it is Hegelian, Kojève's account departs from Hegel's on several important points.

In *On Tyranny*, Kojève argues that along with the satisfaction that comes from the completion of a project, all political struggle is derived from the desire for honor or the recognition of "one's eminent human reality and dignity."[12] The fact that political life is primarily motivated by a desire for recognition does not, Kojève argues, detract from its value or virtue. Instead, Kojève says that a person gains confidence in his understanding of the truth when this truth is validated by others: "It is only by seeing our ideas shared by others . . . or accepted by them as *worth discussing* . . . that we can be sure of not finding ourselves in the realm of madness."[13] Further, Kojève writes, a philosopher would not be satisfied with the confirmation of his thoughts by a select few, as such a group would share common prejudices that could prove detrimental to their common project.[14] Instead, a person in search of wisdom must take himself to the marketplace where he can be confronted with as many and as diverse a set of minds as possible, so as to test his theories adequately.[15] The philosopher, being human, seeks recognition and the desire for recognition furthers his quest for truth. Desiring recognition and the quest for wisdom are not in competition, but complement each other. All humans, Kojève says, desire recognition, and achieving recognition of the correctness of their thoughts confirms to the philosophers that they are on the right path.

As such, the philosopher seeks to have his understanding confirmed by as many individuals as possible. In agreement with Strauss, Kojève notes that the recognition of the philosopher must come from people who are considered capable of fully appreciating his worth.[16] As such, the philosopher will seek to make as many people as possible worthy of recognizing his true value; the philosopher will become a teacher and subsequently enter the political arena, either as an educator of the ruler or as a beneficent tyrant.[17] The recognition of people from a single state among many, however, would still be insufficient. If the desire for recognition speaks to some inherent truth about human beings, then it is only properly expressed and fulfilled when all humans everywhere are recognized and similarly recognize one another. The philosopher statesman would seek not just to rule his own community, but would want to extend the boundaries of that community to an empire or, as Kojève terms it, a world homogenous state. Only a community that embraces all of humanity is capable of fully expressing the truth of human life and satisfying its most significant desire for recognition.[18]

The modern tyrannies that prompted Strauss to reexamine the nature of ancient tyranny in the hopes of awakening the modern world to its crisis, are instead, according to Kojève, proper expressions of a movement to a world homogenous state: "Simonides describes the 'ideal' tyranny, [and] one finds that what might have appeared utopian to Xenophon has nowadays become an almost commonplace reality."[19] In this community, Kojève argues, people will be finally and fully satisfied.

KOJÈVE ON *THE PHENOMENOLOGY OF SPIRIT*

Kojève describes the desire for recognition as the basis for self-consciousness and ultimately human happiness. While this argument is outlined in his responses to Strauss in *On Tyranny*, a more detailed foundation for his argument is found in his treatment of Hegel's *Phenomenology of Spirit*. It is on what he takes to be the strength of Kojève's interpretation that Strauss overlooks the fullness of Hegel's thought as a more adequate defense of the possibilities of modern life.

Kojève's account of the *Phenomenology of Spirit* identifies desire as the means and end of self-consciousness, for, as he notes, "[it is] Desire that generates Self-Consciousness. The human reality—is, finally, a function of the desire for 'recognition.'"[20] The nature of desire, rather than the capacity for thought, Kojève argues, defines human beings in the Hegelian account. Thought alone cannot adequately demonstrate an individual's true nature, for in abstract contemplation, one actually loses consciousness of oneself by contemplating something else.[21] Alternatively, when an individual desires something, he is aware of his desire and himself, thereby becoming an object for his thought.[22] Further and importantly, according to Kojève, when someone recognizes himself by means of his desire, he gains the opportunity to know his true nature. Desire, he writes, is a longing for what one does not have and its presence indicates the fundamental openness of human nature.[23] In confronting desire, people face their insufficiency and mortality. By means of the work that momentarily sustains them, they demonstrate or confirm their identities as beings that negate and will be negated. By transforming the rest of the natural order just as their own nature will be transformed and negated, individuals confirm their understanding in the world. Kojève writes, "the profound basis of Hegelian anthropology is formed by this idea that Man is not a Being that *is* in an eternal identity to itself in Space, but a Nothingness that *nihilates* as Time in spatial Being through the *negation* of this Being—through the negation or transformation of the given."[24] For Kojève, human nature is defined by the understanding that there is nothing essential about human nature; human beings are beings with the capacity to recognize the non-being that is their essence. Humans demonstrate this understanding of non-being by the negating activity of their work in the natural order.

Kojève explains that one cannot immediately achieve this level of self-awareness. As noted, this process begins when individuals recognize their desire; immediate desires, however, are satiated in the consumption of external objects. Once these types of desires are met, individuals lose sight of themselves again and, instead, become defined by the object that just satisfied their need. Self-consciousness, alternatively, requires that one know oneself as an autonomous being, distinguished from all other things. To achieve this, Kojève says, the individual has to desire to be desired by another.[25] In doing this, a person becomes conscious of himself in an ongoing desire that is never satiated. The individual's true nature is, thereby, brought to his attention. In other words, when he receives recognition, or the desire of another, the object that becomes the focus of his thought is the other person animated by desire, the very same desire that animates his own being. In contemplating the desire of another, he comes to know himself. Kojève says, "To desire Being is to fill oneself with this given Being, to enslave oneself to it. To desire non-Being is to liberate oneself from Being, to realize one's autonomy, one's Freedom. . . . Desire must be directed to non-being—that is, toward another *Desire*, another greedy emptiness, another *I*."[26] The desire that is contemplated presents the same openness or emptiness that defines human nature. In contemplating this desire, one finally contemplates one's own being, thereby achieving self-consciousness.

There is, however, the problem of making oneself desirable. According to Kojève, in the earliest stage of human development, the solution lies in the willingness to differentiate oneself from all other animals, in a willingness to face one's own death.[27] Early humans demonstrate their worth by confronting the true nature of their beings and through seeking combat with another. This initial confrontation is unsatisfying as both combatants are either dead or one has surrendered and did not achieve his goal, but is at the same time not suitable to recognize the other's worth, being, himself, worth so much less.[28] This leads to the pivotal relationship, for Kojève, of the master and the slave, wherein the slave, in the moment of his greatest fear and the process of work, truly recognizes and accepts the nothingness that will be his death. He thereby gains a consciousness of himself that is necessary for the progression and eventual end of history.[29]

The slave is a slave because he fears death. In the work that he does for his master, he discovers the nature of freedom. Transforming the products of nature for the satisfaction of another, the slave denies his own desires, thereby transforming himself. He knows he will someday die and his fear of death is initially his motivator. However, he ultimately operates not out of biological necessity, but rather in response to knowledge: "By acting, he negates, he transforms the given, Nature, *his* Nature; and he does so in relation to an *idea* . . . in relation to the idea of a *Master*—i.e., to an essentially *social*, human, historical notion."[30] The slave comes to understand the relationship between the desire that is his nature and his capacity for freedom. The fundamental openness of desire that is at the heart of human nature also reveals that nature as free. In gaining freedom from biological desires, the slave gains the capacity to desire a full manifestation of his being in the world.[31] He desires freedom, and in this journey he further seeks to transform his social and historical situation by means of his work so that, eventually, there are no longer any slaves.

Kojève and Strauss both agree that for Hegel, the desire motivating all progress is the desire for recognition, a phrase that they suggest is synonymous with Hegel's understanding of freedom: "for the desire to be 'recognized' in one's reality and in one's eminent human dignity . . . is actually . . . the ultimate motive of all *emulation* among men and hence all political *struggle*."[32] When this desire has been fully realized, all people, according to Kojève, will accept their mortality and face the necessity of their deaths. Living in a state of authenticity, they are the appropriate objects of desire for others.[33] Put differently, all people will achieve a state wherein their worth and value as autonomous and complete individuals can be recognized by all other autonomous and complete people by means of legally protected rights and freedoms.[34] Having reached the stage of their highest development, all people are recognized as such and given the appropriate freedom to self-govern as their mature sensibilities now dictate.

Kojève further argues that human beings will only achieve the satisfaction that they desire within a world homogenous state. If human beings are only satisfied when their individuality is universally and objectively realized, they will not be satisfied until the state guaranteeing their rights and freedoms is a state that encompasses all possible citizens. Kojève writes, "By fully realizing individuality, the universal and homogenous State completes History."[35] Kojève projects the eventual realization of the perfect empire, wherein all, or at least most, people are recognized as autonomous bearers of rights and correspondingly embrace the principles of the world regime. Kojève further argues that his vision is one that is being realized, for in *On Tyranny*, Kojève notes that utopian states such as those envisioned by Xenophon's Simonides are actually commonplace, citing Salazar's Portugal as an example.[36]

STRAUSS'S ANCIENT CRITIQUE OF MODERNITY

As we shall see in the following chapters, Kojève's interpretation of Hegel is difficult to uphold in light of the full scope of Hegel's thought. Yet it is not on these grounds that Strauss disagrees with Kojève. Instead, Strauss disputes Kojève's account of human nature and its satisfaction, using this disagreement as the springboard from which he goes on to critique modernity more broadly. By implicitly accepting Kojève's account of Hegel, Strauss's critique of Kojève gives one the false impression, intentional or not, that Strauss is responding to Hegel's philosophy in and of itself. Strauss makes four substantial arguments against this Kojève/Hegel hybrid. In brief, Strauss contends that human nature will not be satisfied by Kojève's account of freedom, the more particular desire for recognition, or the world homogenous state. Finally, Strauss pinpoints historicism as the problematic foundation for all of modern thought, particularly that of Hegel. We will look at each of Strauss's criticisms in turn.

Freedom and Passion

The virtues that Strauss has in mind are those of Aristotle's *Ethics*, wherein the gentleman is described as possessing a life that is second only to the philosopher's in terms of its goodness and happiness. From this perspective, seeking to understand the nature of truth and goodness, and attempting to act in a fashion that corresponds with this understanding, is the means to human virtue and happiness. In contrast, the emphasis of the modern world on freedom denigrates all conceptions of duty and is destructive of the possibility of human virtue, and Strauss remarks, in modernity "freedom gradually takes the place of virtue."[37] The prevalent understanding of freedom in the modern western world, Strauss explains, is based solely in passion, and is divorced from any rational determination of what is good or bad. As a result, one can no longer meaningfully speak of another's virtue because freedom means that all potential activities must be counted as equal; no action can thus be decided on as more virtuous than another. The only conceivable virtue or, more aptly, value that might be universally acknowledged as good is the recognition and protection of one's innate freedom. Conceived as such, Strauss argues that human rights provide only an arbitrary moral foundation. He says, "Modern man is a giant in comparison to earlier man. But we have to note that there is no corresponding increase in wisdom or goodness. . . . Nothing can be said about the right use of that immense power. Modern man is a blind giant."[38]

Strauss contrasts modern liberalism with the liberal person of the ancient world:

> the man who behaves in a manner becoming a free man comes to sight primarily as a liberal man in the sense articulated by Aristotle. He knows that certain activities and hence in particular certain sciences and arts—the liberal sciences and arts—are choiceworthy for their own sake, regardless of their utility for the satisfaction of the lower kind of needs. He prefers the goods of the soul to the goods of the body. Liberality is then only one aspect of, not to say one name for, human excellence or being honorable and decent.[39]

The properly liberal or free man, according to Strauss, is a person who escapes from the compulsion of his passions and desires. Rather than being enslaved by the finite nature that defines his body, he governs it with an eye to what is eternally right and good. In the ancient world, Strauss argues, the truly free individual was capable of governing himself in view of what was objectively best. Practically speaking, this meant distancing oneself as far as was possible from the pleasures of the body, recognizing that these pleasures are temporary and more often than not serve to distract from the purer pleasures of the soul. One might recall the image that Socrates offers in the *Republic* of individuals, who like cattle, are ever feasting with their heads focused on the ground, thereby never experiencing the beauty of the heavens that would be available to them if they would only look upward.[40] More specifically, Aristotle delineates a host of ethical virtues, arguing that the most important element for human happiness is to be habituated to what is properly pleasant (virtue) and away from what is painful (vice). Of the ethical virtues, those that are most explicitly concerned with the body—courage, which moderates one's fear of death; and temperance, the moderation of physical desires—are dealt with first, signaling the need to direct one's concerns to the soul rather than the body.[41] Although the philosopher is constrained to live in his body, he is independent of it, and as self-sufficient or as free as is humanly possible. Strauss writes, "The wise man alone is free."[42]

Additionally and important to note in light of our critique of Strauss, in *On Tyranny*, Strauss suggests that a practical or political freedom is also important. Strauss identifies the best possible regime as a regime wherein the rule of law allows for a degree of freedom not possible in a tyranny. Knowing the law, citizens or subjects are freed from the fear of arbitrary intrusions into their lives. Correspondingly, where the law does not speak, these individuals are free to determine themselves. As Strauss notes, virtue that is freely chosen is truer than coerced virtue.[43]

In contrast, Strauss suggests that, for moderns, being free means being free from all obligations, and having rights requires having no corresponding duties. While Aristotle suggested that lawmakers should seek to cultivate at least a habit of virtue in their citizens, the modern legislator seeks only to recognize and protect rights with as little reference as is possible to what one might rightly do with one's freedom. This is the heart of the "last man" notion that so distinguishes the modern account of freedom from the ancient view. The modern man is a last man, it is argued, because there is very little that distinguishes him from any other animal. Unlike the ancient philosopher, or even the gentleman, the last man is concerned only with the maintenance and pleasure of his body, and given the mutable nature of the physical realm, these bodies can be pleased in any number of ways.

Interestingly, Strauss comprehends that Hegel's understanding of freedom transcends the position that being free means being able to do whatever one wants. He insists instead, throughout his lectures, that freedom for Hegel consists of doing what is rational.[44] Explicating this principle, he says, with some accuracy, that acting reasonably, for Hegel, means obeying the law. When a student in the class points out that laws are never wholly reasonable, Strauss, again with accuracy, says that Hegel of course understood that not all laws would be wholly rational. However, he concludes the explanation by saying this "is a very obscure point: Hegel's general tendency to assume a convergence of the is and the ought conceals [the] problem."[45] Strauss leaves the impression that Hegel has no fully reasonable account as to why freedom lies in the obedience of laws, indicating instead that Hegel does not sufficiently take this up, relying instead on his claim: that what is, is as it ought to be. Most troubling in this exchange is that Strauss does not attempt to explain Hegel's point that the actual is rational, but instead says, "*Somehow* Hegel assumes the convergence of the is and the ought, and this assumption is proven as sound by his philosophy of history because it proves that history is rational."[46] One is left with the impression that Strauss takes this "proof" as being less than satisfactory.

One of the reasons Strauss does not more fully engage with Hegel's argument concerning the rational nature of freedom stems from his understanding that Hegel argues that the progress of history depends predominantly on human passion, specifically that of the world-historical individual. Strauss reads the account of Hegel's world-historical individual very narrowly, asserting that the interests that drive such a person to seek to change his society "are the passions, the irrational passions."[47] Correspondingly, in his 1965 lectures on the same topic, Strauss, explaining how the world-historical individual does not know the larger end to which his acts proceed, says that such individuals never look to the common good, but only to their own interests.[48] Although Strauss later admits that Hegel understands not all acts in history are rational, some being due to contingency, others to the perverse or wrong decisions of actors, in speaking of the ill effects of the activity of the world-historical figure, no such moments are admitted. Instead, Strauss incorporates all of the activity of the world-historical individual within Hegel's definition of rational, including and perhaps especially, clearly criminal and horrific acts, saying, "when we look at history we see that these world-historical individuals treat human beings all the time as mere means and therefore they are utterly immoral. Thus we are presented with the paradoxy that the rationality of the historical process exists not despite the immorality, but by virtue of that immorality. A most shocking teaching!"[49] While Strauss understands that Hegel claims that his account of freedom is one that is inclusive of and dependent on rational activity, he indicates that the means Hegel espouses, selfish passion, cannot be conducive to any rational end. Thus elsewhere he says, "Hegel's fundamental teaching regarding the master and slave is based on Hobbes' doctrine of the state of nature."[50] And "The right order may have been as loftily conceived by Hegel as it was by Plato, which one may doubt. It certainly was thought by Hegel to be established in the Machiavellian way, not in the Platonic way: it was thought to be established in a manner which contradicted the right order itself."[51] If the course of history allows for and even necessitates the selfish pursuit of human desires, it seems to make no sense to assume that at the end of this quest, individuals will be willing to put their own selfish pursuits aside for the sake of the common good. As such, the freedom that Hegel's philosophy aspires to will be as bogged down in irrational desire as that understood by Hobbes. In the chapters that follow we will address how Hegel's understanding of human desire, and its place within his idea of an ethical community, differs from this portrayal.

The Desire for Recognition

Strauss's second but connected point of disagreement with Kojève's view of political life is whether recognition, even universally granted, will sufficiently satisfy human beings. According to Strauss, it is the philosopher, not the citizen, who has the happiest life, and Strauss, unlike Hegel and Kojève, does not think these two types can be coterminous.

Kojève, in agreement with Hegel, argues that our political reality is an objective confirmation of what is understood as true.[52] The reconciliation of thought with politically active living further confirms that what is subjectively believed about human beings is true of their objective reality. For, "the philosopher cannot give up on pedagogy; in fact, the 'success' with his philosophical pedagogy is the sole 'objective' criterion of the truth of the philosopher's doctrine: the fact of his having disciples. . . . Is his guarantee against the danger of lunacy."[53] Kojève argues that there is a necessary dialectic between the political world that people are a part of and their capacity for self-consciousness. The solitary individual, working in isolation from all others, cannot achieve wisdom. Even the philosopher is subject to the need for recognition. When he desires wisdom, the philosopher also knows that his understanding of the truth requires its confirmation by other thinking beings.[54] The philosopher requires the community not merely for his philosophical well-being but also for his intellectual satisfaction.

While recognizing a dialectical relationship between reason and desire, Kojève clearly emphasizes desire over reason as fundamental to human nature. It is only when a person confronts his nature as essentially defined by desire that he recognizes the openness of his being and his fundamental freedom. Even Kojève's philosopher seeks wisdom not for its own sake, but for the recognition that will follow from being wise. He writes, "nothing prevents us from asserting that, when 'Socrates' *communicates* with others and exercises his virtue *publicly*, he does so not only for the purpose of testing himself but also (and perhaps even above all) for the sake of outward 'recognition.'" In achieving "wisdom," Kojève's philosopher knows the essential truth—human beings exist in a state of utter freedom with the only limit being the recognition of this truth by others.

Strauss disagrees. First, the philosopher and the citizen, or gentleman, are not the same people. Kojève's argument that the life of wisdom is necessarily a political life is premised, according to Strauss, on the idea that the highest thing to know is the self (or human nature).[55] If the end of one's knowledge includes human things, then one should be able to find confirmation of these truths in and through human life. If we accept Kojève's point that the highest of things is human life, and knowledge of this life is indeed fully possible, then it is also possible for the life of the wisest person to correspond with the life of the citizen as both have the same object of interest. Not self-sufficient, human beings are constrained to live in political communities. If a human life is the highest object of thought, then there is no reason for the philosopher to not also be the perfect citizen.

Strauss alternatively argues that as the philosopher is "chiefly concerned with eternal beings or the 'ideas,' and hence also with the 'idea' of man, he is as unconcerned as possible with individual and perishable human beings and hence also with his own 'individuality,' or his body, as well as with the sum total of all human individual human beings and their 'historical' procession."[56] Not seeking to understand himself as a particular person, but rather focusing on that which is eternal, the philosopher must distance himself as far as possible from the everyday concerns of the city and its members. Although the human soul is as close to the transcendent as possible, and therefore something the philosopher strives to understand, the closer this soul moves to perfection, the less it is like any particular human being.[57] Aristotle, therefore, writes that no human actually wishes for his friends to become gods, because at this point they could no longer be his friends.[58] Moreover, as we will see in the next chapter, Strauss argues that the difference between what is metaphysically true and what is physically apparent is such that, while humans are perhaps able to understand something of their own natures and ends, they will not be able to garner any conclusive knowledge of the most important of things. He writes,

> knowledge of the ends of human life . . . is knowledge of what makes human life complete or whole; it is therefore knowledge of a whole. Knowledge of the ends of man implies knowledge of the human soul; and the human soul is the only part of the whole which is open to the whole and therefore more akin to the whole than anything else. But this knowledge—the political art in the highest sense—is not knowledge of *the* whole . . . Men are . . . constantly tempted to force the issue by imposing unity on the phenomena . . . Philosophy is characterized by the gentle, if firm, refusal to succumb.[59]

While the philosopher seeks knowledge of the highest things, he knows that this knowledge is always incomplete. Therefore, the philosopher lives in a limbo-like existence. Necessity confines him to the political community and the limited knowledge that he can thereby gain, but this world and its knowledge are not his actual concern. Subsequently, his real desire for wisdom will never be met. Ultimately, for Strauss, the life of the philosopher may be the same as the life of the political philosopher, but the political philosopher is not a politician and may not even, properly speaking, be a very good citizen. Strauss's philosopher cannot be satisfied by political and civil recognition of his personhood. His only satisfaction, argues Strauss, is found in wisdom, something that is unattainable within the political world and often in conflict with politics. While a gentleman, one who seeks the secondary life of ethical virtue, is initially at least motivated by the desire for honor and seeks to be recognized by some, Strauss suggests that few people have the souls of gentlemen.

Interestingly, Hegel's position shows some similarity to the arguments of both Kojève and Strauss. Like Hegel, Kojève argues that the phenomenal world is a means to knowledge. While Kojève limits the possibility of what can be known to the natural and human realms, Hegel believes that the existence of historical phenomena can be a means to a fuller awareness of the nature of Spirit itself. Hegel's argument suggests that our political existence can reveal human nature and thereby the shared nature of Spirit. This is possible, according to Hegel, because Spirit manifests its nature in the development of human consciousness. While Strauss would disagree with the idea that a particular human life is capable of revealing the nature of the divine in any full way, Hegel's thought does concur with Strauss's in that he sees the need for philosophy to extend beyond the particular to the universal.

World Homogenous State

Kojève posits the world homogenous state as the ultimate outcome of Hegel's political thought. Importantly, Strauss understands that the world homogenous state is not the ethical community to which Hegel himself points. However, in his 1958 lectures, Strauss seems to accept that the global community projected by Kojève is the logical and necessary outcome of Hegelian thought when applied in the modern era. Unfortunately, there is a break in the audiotape leading up to Strauss's remarks on Kojève and so we do not know what it is explicitly about modernity that Strauss believes makes Hegel's idea of particular and differentiated ethical communities an implausible option; however, his comments indicate that it is in reference to the disintegration of the constitutional monarchies and the emergence of purely popular governments. Exactly why Strauss believes that only a world homogenous state would be the logical development or only alternative to the constitutional monarchy presented by Hegel is left unsaid. However, Strauss does say that in the idea of the world homogenous state Kojève "presents the . . . solution as the transformation of Hegel which is indispensible" and "what Hegel groped after was a universal state."[60]

Strauss disagrees with Kojève, if not Hegel, on the point that human aspirations will be satisfied by a world homogenous state. The fullness of this disagreement is revealed in Strauss and Kojève's correspondence on Xenophon's *Hiero*. In *Hiero*, a discussion about the life of a tyrant turns to a discussion about the relative value of the political life versus the philosophical life. Central to the argument is the comparative nature and worth of *love* versus *admiration*. It is here that we most clearly see Strauss's disagreement with Kojève on the value and credibility of a world empire. On the question of love and admiration, Strauss says to the extent that the philosopher cares for either, he would always choose admiration over love. Alternatively, Strauss argues that the political person who is at the heart of Kojève's interpretation of Hegel seeks not "recognition" but rather love, or at least, Strauss tells us, this is the view of Xenophon's *Hiero.* Love, Strauss says, is based not on what one has done, but rather on the fact that one is. A person loves what is his own regardless of what other traits, admirable or despicable, the object of his love might have. A mother is supposed to always love her children regardless of what they accomplish. Admiration or honor, however, is granted on the basis of what one has accomplished. People are properly honored only when they are honorable. Comparing admiration to love, Strauss says, "Admiration is as much superior to love as the man of excellence is to one's benefactor as such. . . . Love has no criteria of its relevance outside of itself, but admiration has."[61] Being honorable depends on excellence and very few people, Strauss argues, are capable of the virtue that would make them truly worthy of the honor of others.[62] Further, he says, the person who bestows honor must be worthy of doing so. This person must be capable of judging one's characteristics as honorable and, thus, he must be of a similar nature. In contrast, when people crave love, they are not concerned about the nature of the source, merely the effect. Just as there will be few honorable people, there are just as few people who are worthy of granting this honor.

While Strauss ultimately believes that honor is not the desired end of the truly excellent person or the philosopher, he also says that it is an important (if not necessary) mechanism for encouraging people to begin their paths to excellence. In a particularly Strauss-like demonstration of this argument in Xenophon's *Hiero*, Strauss writes:

> The wise man is as self-sufficient as is humanly possible; the admiration which he gains is essentially a tribute to his perfection, and not a reward for any services. The desire for praise and admiration as distinguished from the desire for love is the natural foundation for the predominance of the desire for one's own perfection. This is what Xenophon subtly indicates by presenting Simonides chiefly as interested in the pleasures of eating, whereas Hiero appears to be chiefly interested in the pleasures of sex: for the enjoyment of food, as distinguished from sexual enjoyments, one does not need other people.[63]

By showing his preference for food, Simonides demonstrates that he is suited to the life of virtue and ultimately philosophy. This life is one wherein the greater a person's excellence, the fewer compliments he requires by the small number of people capable of bestowing them. More than the desire for recognition, the philosopher desires wisdom regardless of the honor granted and in spite of the fact that the truly philosophic soul knows that there will be next to no one with whom he can share his accomplishments.

Unlike Strauss, Kojève argues that the political person, wanting to be recognized for his true worth, seeks honor, not love. Accepting that this is true for a moment, Strauss still rejects the possibility that this person will be satisfied with the world homogenous state. Such a community implies mutual universal recognition or the admiration of everyone for and by everyone else. The existence of such a community, Strauss argues, requires either the dubious possibility that everyone has attained wisdom and excellence or, and more likely, that the possibilities for human excellence have been so diluted that everyone is capable of achieving it.[64] Regardless, Strauss does not agree that the tyrant is motivated by the desire for honor and he does not imagine that most people are gentlemen. Instead, Strauss believes that tyrants and most other human beings seek love, and this selfish obsession has a negative impact on virtue.[65] As there would be little reason for anyone to seek true excellence in a world homogenous state, such a community, Strauss suggests, would be a very dreary place to live. We can perhaps more easily see Strauss's point in Kojève's account of the "last man." Kojève writes:

> In the final state there naturally are no more 'human beings' in our sense of an *historical* human being. The 'healthy' automata are 'satisfied' (sports, arts, eroticism, etc.) and the 'sick' ones get locked up. As for those who are not satisfied with their 'purposeless activity' (art, etc.) they are the philosophers (who can attain wisdom if they 'contemplate' enough). By doing so they become 'gods.' The tyrant becomes an administrator, a cog in the 'machine' fashioned by automata for automata.[66]

In seeming response, Strauss says, "it is perhaps possible to say that the universal and homogenous state is fated to come. But it is certainly impossible to say that man can be reasonably satisfied with it. If the universal and homogenous state is the goal of History, History is absolutely 'tragic.'"[67]

According to Strauss, the implementation of the world homogenous state would only occur at the hands of a tyrant, an ironic conclusion given that the world state, for Kojève, arises from a desire for freedom. Whether Strauss thought that this tyranny would most likely exist in the form of the explicit terror experienced under Hitler or Stalin or the more benign, but, in his view, similarly destructive, kind of tyranny envisioned by Tocqueville is unclear. What is clear is Strauss's belief that in such a state, no one, not even the tyrant, could ever be satisfied or happy.

In those developments that Kojève would likely see as progress, such as the pressures of globalization and the creation of the European Union, Strauss would presumably view as detrimental to human satisfaction and/or doomed to failure. The homogenizing effects of globalization point not to a more complete realization of justice or human happiness, but rather to the lowering standards of each. In such a world, the possibility of true virtue and philosophy is diminished, for each depends on proper habituation. Instead, left to the fulfillment of their desires, most people will fulfill those desires that are most immediately pleasant.

Historicism

Hegel argues that human knowledge, as a whole, develops historically. Just as children must learn basic math before they learn calculus, Hegel argues that human consciousness progresses in time to a greater and greater awareness of the true. However, in looking back over the grand sweep of history, Strauss does not see a progressive development in human understanding, or any fundamental improvement in social and political orders. Instead, Strauss argues, history offers us nothing but chaotic change: "To the unbiased historian, 'the historical process' revealed itself as the meaningless web spun by what men did, produced and thought, no more than by unmitigated chance—a tale told by an idiot."[68] Strauss concludes that the "great advancements" of science and liberal democratic regimes have not led to creating more thoughtful and virtuous people. Having achieved greater and greater freedom from the limits of nature and law, human beings have sought to primarily fulfill their base and, most often, corrupt desires. Strauss argues that this development is the logical outcome of Hegel's philosophy.

Strauss outlines this development within the discipline of political science. Aristotle claimed that political science was the master of all practical sciences because it determined the proper scope of human activities on the basis of what was thought to be most conducive to a good human life.[69] In contrast, modern political science can no longer speak of the good or the bad. Science must be value free, refraining from making normative claims about better or worse activity and, instead, occupying itself with the task of measuring quantifiable behavior. Strauss connects this development directly to Hegel:

> Hegel's demand that political philosophy refrain from construing a state as it ought to be, or from teaching a state how it should be, and that it try to understand the present and actual state as something essentially rational, amounts to a rejection of the *raison d'etre* of classical political philosophy. The attempt to replace the quest for the best political order by a purely descriptive or analytical political science which refrains from 'value judgments' is, from the point of view of the classics, as absurd as the attempt to replace the art of making shoes . . . [with] a museum of shoes made by apprentices, or as the idea of medicine which refuses to distinguish between health and sickness.[70]

The political philosopher is replaced by the statistician who measures human activities, but is never able to tell whether the activities in question are good or bad. According to this argument, if a person can only understand the period in which he lives and is unable to grasp any absolute truth, the political philosopher's role becomes to collect historical data. However, no judgments can sensibly be made about whether the collected results are good or bad.

This account of Hegel is only partially correct. Hegel does say that the role of the philosopher is to understand what *is* rather than what one might wish would be.[71] In this, however, Hegel is far from arguing for a value-free political science. Hegel's point, instead, is that the political world we create and inhabit takes up the nature of Spirit and the nature of the good in and for itself. As such, the current world as well as those that preceded it, and those that will follow it, are rational expositions of the truth. This does not mean that these political orders are perfect or that every element of their existence is reasonably defined. Political life will always admit of the contingencies that pervade the finite world. However, insofar as they exist, they are rational, something even Plato would agree with and the role of the philosopher is to discern what is rational within them.[72]

In his lectures, Strauss allows these points, indicating to his students that in saying that the actual is rational, Hegel is not thereby saying that everything that exists is therefore rational. The accidental, the contingent, the immoral, and criminal are all present, Strauss says, in Hegel's account of the end of history.[73] It is only the decisive or fundamental acts that are rational, he claims. However, even allowing for these caveats, Strauss remains unconvinced of Hegel's account of history's reason. In some respects it is Hegel's recognition of the place of chance in history that Strauss finds problematic. Strauss suggests that when things do not proceed rationally within history, Hegel gives himself a rather convenient out. For example, Strauss writes, "Look at Hitler's program; look at his obsession with the Jewish question . . . [F]or the Germans, and especially for the Jews in Germany, this accident was not a marginal thing but decisive in importance. There is a certain inhumanity in this way of looking at things."[74] Hegel, Strauss implies, can merely chalk such atrocities up to accident and wait for the next rational development that proves his thesis. If this account of history is rational, then reason must be immoral.

In addition to the difficulties that Strauss has with Hegel's specific account of history, he finds even more problematic the influence that Hegel's thought has on subsequent philosophers. Although Hegel could not convince the philosophic world that he had seen the absolute moment of history and thus truth, he did convince the philosophers that followed him that all knowledge is historically determined.

The political results of this philosophic temperament are necessarily diverse. Ancient philosophy demanded that the virtuous seek a rationally understood common good, thereby leading Socrates to declare that a just person seeks the good of all, harming neither his friends nor his enemies.[75] In ancient thought, while determining what might be good within a given set of circumstances may have been difficult, if not impossible, there was at least the general acceptance that such a good existed, and that it should govern one's actions. The authentic existentialist has no such basis for his relationship with others.

The statement that all truth is historically relative is equivalent to saying that there is no absolute truth. However, to say that there is no truth is to say that *this* statement is in fact the only truth, and the person who understands this fact has a claim on wisdom or authenticity. This person lives every moment understanding that there is no meaning behind or in front of his activity except what he determines for it. According to this argument, the majority of humans live in the false security provided by the façade of their historical situation. The truly authentic person needs no such illusions. Such individuals may decide to be charitable to those unable to withstand the pressures of their angst or they may not. In the end, the decision is theirs, and political life is left without any determinative philosophic guide. Speaking of Heidegger who, for Strauss, defines existentialism, Strauss says:

> There is no room for political philosophy in Heidegger's work, and this may well be due to the fact that the room in question is occupied by gods or the gods. This does not mean that Heidegger is wholly alien to politics: he welcomed Hitler's revolution in 1933 and he . . . praised national socialism long after Hitler had been muted. . . . We cannot help but hold these facts against Heidegger. Moreover, one is bound to misunderstand Heidegger's thought radically if one does not see their intimate connection with the core of his philosophic thought.[76]

Regardless of what one thinks of Heidegger's association with National Socialism, Strauss clearly saw a direct line with the nihilism associated with postmodern thought and the political horrors of the twentieth century.

More than just being naïve or incorrect, Hegel's philosophy, for Strauss, has to be seen as philosophically and politically destructive. Hegel's work destroys not only the possibility of the best human life—the life of the philosopher—but also the possibility that most humans might live even fairly good lives. Semantics such as these no longer make sense. Strauss seeks to point human beings in general, or at least those who are noble, in a better direction. Rather than looking to the future, according to Strauss, individuals should look to the past. Insofar as the truth is eternal, and the ancient world was not plagued with the historical problems of the modern, then one might derive an alternative and even superior way to think and live from the ancient account.[77]

Despite Strauss's obvious preference for things ancient, he also writes sympathetically about the work of Nietzsche, a philosopher firmly rooted in the tradition of existential thought and perhaps the first influential thinker to transform Hegel's historicism to the more radical version that Strauss describes. Accepting the relative nature of all truth, Nietzsche argues that this understanding is destructive to most people: "individuality . . . shaken, and left without any sure belief in itself; it sinks into its own inner being, which means here only the disordered chaos of what it has learned, which will never express itself externally, being mere dogma that cannot be turned to life. Looking further, we see how the banishment of instinct by history has turned men into shades and abstractions."[78] Seeing the potentially disastrous consequences of this position, Nietzsche seeks to find a philosophic foothold for human beings, a foothold that has a value not just as a philosophic system, but also for life.

Nietzsche suggests it is the work of great individuals to consciously seize the historically constructed nature of truth and consciously build historical horizons themselves in order to reinvigorate human belief and activity. The basis for such a creative enterprise is left, however, deliberatively vague, and as Strauss writes, "We can do no more than allude here to the difficulties that afflict his situation. I have in mind . . . whether he did not . . . try to find a sufficient theoretical basis for a transhistorical teaching or message."[79] If there are no universal and transhistorical truths, it is unclear where one is to find the foundation for the walls of Nietzsche's new horizons.

Regardless of Nietzsche's radical relativism, Strauss finds his thought to be a hopeful response to the problems perceived in Hegel's emphasis on the philosophy of history. By confronting and revealing the fully relativistic nature of history, Nietzsche, Strauss tells us, demonstrates that the foundation for human life cannot come from a study of history. Whether intended by Nietzsche or not, the result of his thought, according to Strauss, is an ancient one: in order for the individual to find truth, he must turn from the study of history, which has revealed itself as mere convention, to nature—forgetting that, from Nietzsche's perspective, "nature" must be just as mythical as the possibility of a progressive history.[80]

Choosing the relativism of Nietzsche over the teleological historicism of Hegel would appear to be an odd choice for a thinker like Strauss to make, particularly when Strauss himself notes that Nietzsche's clarification of historicism as radical relativism concludes in the existentialism of Heidegger. And yet, Strauss suggests that despite this ultimate result, Nietzsche's thought is preferable to the radical historicism that Strauss perceives Hegel's philosophy creating. For, as Strauss consoles:

> [T]here is no reason for despair as long as human nature has not been conquered completely, i.e., as long as sun and man will still generate man. There will always be men who will revolt against a state which is destructive of humanity or in which there is no longer a possibility of noble actions and great deeds. They may be forced into a mere negation of the world homogenous state, a negation not enlightened by any positive goal, into a nihilistic negation. While perhaps doomed to fail-

> ure, the nihilistic revolution may be the only action on behalf of man's humanity and the only great and noble deed that is possible.[81]

We are left to speculate what the nature of such a revolution might look like and what Strauss thinks the consequences of such an event will be.[82]

Strauss seeks to lead the reader back to what he considers is firmer ground, where human virtue rather than license determines one's intellectual, social, and political life. By studying political philosophy, rather than the history of political thought, Strauss believes the individual will be led to understand that the very problems he grapples with—the justice of war, the relevance of the family to the state, the problem of political apathy—are the very questions that all political philosophers have tried to understand and answer. And, "if the fundamental problems persist in all historical change, human thought is capable of transcending its historical limitation or of grasping something trans-historical. This would be the case even if it were true that all attempts to solve these problems are doomed to fail and that they are doomed to fail on account of the 'historicity' of 'all' human thought."[83] Ultimately, Strauss suggests that the emptiness of nihilism, and perhaps even the political terrors that this philosophic position accepts, may be what is required for human beings to be shaken from the lull that a surfeit of historical understanding has encouraged in them.

Strauss perceives the plight of the modern world with pessimism; humans have embraced absolute freedom as their end and, as such, perceive any external limitation on their activity as arbitrary. Further, Strauss pinpoints Hegel as the source of this error. Strauss finds Hegel's historical thesis so destructive that he takes solace in the very corruption that breeds his desperation; the nihilism of the modern age may result in such politically destructive acts that human beings will be forced to confront the political philosophy that they have so unquestionably accepted. This critique and the possible solutions suggested by Strauss only hold, however, if Hegel's philosophy does not contain a response to the problems that Strauss sees as emanating from modernity. We contend that Hegel foresaw the problems that Strauss's interpretation of his thought points to and, further, that Hegel suggests an alternative solution.

Agreeing with Strauss, we are concerned by Kojève's easy acceptance of actual tyrants. And, like Strauss, we find the image of Kojève's last men, or automata, disheartening if not terrifying.[84] Agreeing with Kojève, however, we are put off by the seeming "aristocratic prejudice" that Strauss's small philosophic circle suggests. And with Kojève, we are disheartened by Strauss's affinity to an ancient world wherein only a handful of individuals were deemed worthy of political and civil rights. The problem, however, lies in the dichotomy that Strauss has constructed.

Ultimately, Strauss's return to the ancient world, or Kojève's world homogenous state, are not the only options open to us. Hegel's philosophy, although misappropriated by Kojève, if read in full, offers another alternative—an alternative that does not see merely a debate between the ancient and modern world, but rather, a way to reconcile the best elements of each. In brief, we intend to show that the strengths that Strauss perceives in the ancient world are present in Hegel's account and, at the same time, the advantages that Kojève (and even Strauss) inevitably regarded as being present in liberal democratic states are further solidified and supported by Hegel. For as Stanley Rosen, a student of both Strauss and Kojève, writes of Hegel, "every effort is made to preserve the wisdom of the ancients. If this wisdom is transformed in its ascent to a higher level, it nevertheless transforms by its presence the character of modern wisdom as well."[85] In Hegel's account, modernity is not opposed to antiquity but rather incorporates the strengths of the ancients and reconciles these to itself.

NOTES

1. Gourevitch, "Philosophy and Politics," I, 59.
2. Leo Strauss. Papers [Box 9, Folder 2], Special Collections Research Center, University of Chicago Library.
3. Leo Strauss to Alexandre Kojève, April 8, 1947, in *On Tyranny*, 236.
4. Alexander Kojève to Leo Strauss, May 26, 1949, in *On Tyranny*, 241.
5. For an interesting account of the contrast in motivations between Strauss and Kojève, see Robert Pippin, "Being, Time, and Politics: The Strauss-Kojève Debate," *History and Theory* 32:2 (May, 1993): 148.
6. Strauss, "On Tyranny," in *On Tyranny*, 23–24.
7. Strauss, "Restatement," in *On Tyranny*, 196.
8. Strauss, "On Tyranny," in *On Tyranny* 28–29.
9. Ibid., 24.
10. Gourevitch, "Philosophy and Politics," I, 75.
11. Kojève, "Tyranny and Wisdom," in *On Tyranny*, 152.
12. Ibid., 143.
13. Ibid., 153.
14. Ibid., 154–55.
15. Ibid., 155. See also, Strauss, "Restatement," in *On Tyranny*, 205.
16. Strauss, "On Tyranny," in *On Tyranny*, 88, and Kojève, "Tyranny and Wisdom," in *On Tyranny*, 157.
17. Kojève, "Tyranny and Wisdom," in *On Tyranny*, 156–58 and 162–63.
18. Ibid., 145–46.
19. Ibid., 138.
20. Kojève, *Introduction to the Reading of Hegel: Lectures on the* Phenomenology of Spirit, ed. Allan Bloom (New York: Cornell University Press, 1969), 7.
21. Ibid., 3.
22. Ibid., 3–4.
23. Ibid., 5.
24. Ibid., 48.
25. Ibid., 6–7.
26. Ibid., 40.
27. Ibid., 39–40.

28. Ibid., 46.
29. Ibid., 47, 56–57.
30. Ibid., 48.
31. Ibid., 4–5.
32. Kojève, "Tyranny and Wisdom," in *On Tyranny*, 151.
33. Kojève, *Introduction to the Reading of Hegel*, 43–44.
34. Kojève, "Tyranny and Wisdom," in *On Tyranny*, 171–74.
35. Kojève, *Introduction to the Reading of Hegel*, 237. See also, Kojève, "Tyranny and Wisdom," in *On Tyranny*, 145 and 157.
36. Kojève, "Tyranny and Wisdom," in *On Tyranny*, 138–39.
37. Strauss, "Progress and Return," in *On Tyranny*, 271.
38. Ibid., 239.
39. Leo Strauss, "The Liberalism of Classical Political Philosophy," *The Review of Metaphysics* 12:3 (March, 1959): 393.
40. Plato, *The Republic*," 586a.
41. Aristotle, *The Nicomachean Ethics* (Indianapolis: Hackett Publishing Co., 2000).
42. Strauss, "On Tyranny," in *On Tyranny*, 87.
43. Ibid., 72.
44. Leo Strauss. Papers [Box 9, Folder 2], Special Collections Research Center, University of Chicago Library.
45. Ibid.
46. Ibid.
47. Leo Strauss. Papers [Box 9, Folder 1], Special Collections Research Center, University of Chicago Library.
48. Leo Strauss, "Seminar in Political Philosophy: Hegel's *The Philosophy of History*" (lecture, The Leo Strauss Centre, leostrausscenter.uchicago.edu, May 1, 1965).
49. Ibid.
50. Strauss, "A Restatement," in *On Tyranny*, 205. See also, Leo Strauss, "An Introduction to Political Philosophy," in *An Introduction to Political Philosophy* ed. Hilael Gilden (Detroit: Wayne State University Press, 1989); and Leo Strauss, *The Political Philosophy of Hobbes* (Chicago: University of Chicago Press, 1996), 56–57.
51. Strauss, "An Introduction to Political Philosophy," in *An Introduction to Political Philosophy*, 56.
52. Kojève, *Introduction to the Reading of Hegel*, 95, 237.
53. Kojève, "Tyranny and Wisdom," in *On Tyranny*, 173.
54. Ibid., 153–55.
55. Strauss, "A Restatement," in *On Tyranny*, 198.
56. Ibid., 212.
57. Ibid., 215–16. See also Zuckert, *The Truth About Leo Strauss*, 174.
58. Aristotle, *Nicomachean Ethics* (Indianapolis: Hackett Publishing Co., 2000),1159a, 10.
59. Strauss, "What is Political Philosophy," in *What is Political Philosophy*, 40.
60. Leo Strauss. Papers [Box 9, Folder 2], Special Collections Research Center, University of Chicago Library.
61. Strauss, "On Tyranny," in *On Tyranny*, 92.
For an excellent comment on this account of love, see Robert Pippin, "Being, Time, and Politics: The Strauss-Kojève Debate," *History and Theory* 32:2 (May, 1993): 155.
62. Some scholars have noted the idiosyncratic nature of Strauss's account of love. See, for example, Gourevitch, "Philosophy and Politics," I, 76–77.
63. Strauss, "On Tyranny," in *On Tyranny*, 93.
64. For a clear account of Strauss's understanding of the natural inequality that exists between human beings, see Robb A. McDaniel, "The Nature of Inequality: Uncovering the Modern in Leo Strauss's Idealist Ethics," *Political Theory* 26:3 (June, 1998): 317–45.
65. Strauss, "Restatement," in *On Tyranny*, 202.
66. Kojève to Strauss, September 19, 1950 in *On Tyranny*, 255.

67. Strauss, "A Restatement," in *On Tyranny*, 223. Although he subsequently modifies his argument, Fukuyama's *The End of History* draws out the implications of Strauss's points in this regard. See Francis Fukuyama, *The End of History and the Last Man* (New York: Harper Perennial, 1993), 287–306, 311.

68. Strauss, "Natural Rights and the Historical Approach," in *Natural Right and History* (Chicago: University of Chicago Press, 1953), 18.

69. Aristotle, *Nicomachean Ethics*, 1094a, 27–30.

70. Strauss, "On Classical Political Philosophy," in *What is Political Philosophy?*, 71–72.

71. Hegel, *Elements of the Philosophy of Right*, Preface, 20–23.

72. For example, see Plato, *The Republic*, 508b–509c.

73. Leo Strauss. Papers [Box 9, Folder 2], Special Collections Research Center, University of Chicago Library.

74. Ibid.

75. Plato, *Republic*, trans. G.M.A. Grube (Indianapolis: Hackett Publishing Co., 1992), 335d.

76. Strauss, "Philosophy as Rigorous Science," in *Studies in Platonic Philosophy*, 30.

77. Strauss, "On Classical Political Philosophy," in *What is Political Philosophy?*, 49–71, 78–94; Strauss, "Progress and Return," in *The Rebirth of Classical Political Rationalism*, 249, 310.

78. Nietzsche, *On the Advantage and Disadvantage of History for Life*, trans. Peter Preuss (Indianapolis: Hackett Publishing Co., 1980), 29, sect. 5.

79. Strauss, "Relativism," in *The Rebirth of Classical Political Rationalism*, 26.

80. Ibid.

81. Strauss, "Restatement," in *On Tyranny*, 223–24.

82. For an extreme account about Strauss's relationship to nihilism see Altman, *The German Stranger*.

83. Strauss, "Natural Right and the Historical Approach," in *Natural Right and History*, 114.

84. Kojève to Strauss, September 19, 1950 in *On Tyranny*, 255. For an account of how one might view the contemporary world on the basis of Kojève's assumptions, see Barry Cooper, *The End of History: An Essay on Modern Hegelianism* (Toronto: University of Toronto Press, 1984). See also Roth, "A Problem of Recognition: Alexander Kojève and the End of History," *History and Theory* 24: 3 (October, 1985).

85. Stanley Rosen, *G.W.F. Hegel* (New York: Yale University Press, 1974), 10, 11.

TWO

Faith and Reason

The Strauss-Kojève debate focuses on a perceived conflict between antiquity and modernity. The ancient world, Strauss understands, is superior to the modern in that it seeks to orient human beings within a larger whole, directing their attention to an objective good. Kojève alternatively embraces modernity as a purely secular enterprise wherein the only objective truth is the progress of human activity in history. In framing the debate in this way, ancients versus moderns, Strauss and Kojève overlook a very important middle ground, or what Hegel considers the center represented by Christianity.

Hegel interprets Christianity as reconciling the strengths of the ancient and modern worlds, for in it, he argues, knowledge of objective truth is reconciled with individual freedom. Hegel thereby describes Christianity as "the religion of *truth* and the religion of *freedom*."[1] Hegel argues that by means of the revelation of the natural order, the Bible, and finally, Christ, Spirit demonstrates the fullness of its nature to human beings. In so fully making itself manifest, Spirit enables the completion of philosophy or the attainment of wisdom. Further, as a result of this knowledge, people are able to will what they objectively desire and achieve the type of freedom only contemplated by the ancients.

It must be clearly stated that the Christianity referred to by Hegel is widely regarded as unorthodox, at best. In his separation of representational religion from the concept of the Absolute, Hegel raises many questions regarding what is left of the religious dogma of that particular faith. His account is certainly quite different from many contemporary forms of Christianity, particularly in their conservative forms. Yet there is inescapable evidence in Hegel's writings, and particularly in his *Lectures on the Philosophy of Religion*, delivered late in his life, that much of the traditional representational language of orthodox Trinitarian Christianity is consistent with his philosophical position. For the purposes of this argument, the extent of Hegel's divergence from orthodoxy (whatever that may be) is not our concern. What is essential, however, is whether Hegel affirms the existence of a transcendent first principle that is not reduced to human self-consciousness. While recognizing the strength of the argument that focuses on the development of self-consciousness in humanity, we will argue that Hegel also posits a transcendent principle that is the end of this development for human beings.[2]

By providing an objective basis for modern manifestations of individual freedom, Hegel understands Christian theology as serving a foundation for modern political life. As Hegel says:

> To posit . . . principles of freedom is to assert that they are true because they cohere with the innermost self-consciousness of human beings. But if in fact it is reason that discovers these principles, then, to the extent they are genuine . . . it has their verification only in virtue of the fact that it traces them back to the cognition of absolute truth . . . but this cognition must be carried out fully and must go right back to the ultimate analysis . . . but if it does go right to the ultimate ground, it arrives at what is recognized as the highest, or as God.[3]

According to Hegel, the western world's emphasis on subjectivity, freedom, and equality emerges from the Christian understanding of the Absolute, saying of Christianity, "Before God all humans are equal. This comes to consciousness for the first time here and now, in the speculative and negative [elements] of the infinite anguish of love; herein lies the possibility and the root of truly universal justice and of the actualization of freedom."[4] Exactly what Hegel means in this quotation will be taken up in greater detail later in this chapter. Suffice to say, it is our argument that it is these principles that Strauss finds distasteful about modern political life.

Strauss, closely following Kojève, rejects the argument that Hegel's thought is compatible with a Christian account. In brief, he charges that Hegel takes God out of religion. Strauss writes:

> For Hegel the historical process was a rational and reasonable process, a progress, culminating in the rational state. . . . Christianity is the true or absolute religion, but Christianity consists in its reconciliation with the world. . . . It is complete secularization. . . In the case of Hegel we are indeed compelled to say that the essence of modernity is secularized Christianity, for secularization is Hegel's conscious and explicit intention.[5]

Kojève puts it more boldly:

> According to Hegel, one can realize the Christian anthropological ideal only by "overcoming" the Christian theology: Christian Man can really become what he would like to be only by becoming a man without God—or if you will a God-man. He must realize in himself what at first

> he thought was realized in his God. To be really Christian, he himself must become Christ.[6]

In agreement with much contemporary scholarship, both Strauss and Kojève argue that Hegel reduces Christianity to a purely human enterprise, such that the absolute, understood as an objective and universal entity, is reduced to elements of human reason.[7]

Strauss thereby rejects the possibility that Hegel's account is ultimately compatible with Christianity or, perhaps more importantly for him, a life of faith more broadly. He further suggests that Christianity, at least as it is taken up in modern philosophic accounts, undermines the possibility of a genuine philosophic or ethical life for most people. The assumption that human beings are by nature free suggests to Strauss, and indeed to many moderns, that there are no proper limits on human behavior. And a fundamental equality among humans means that acts of excellence are unnoticed or discouraged. In Strauss's account, Machiavelli, Hobbes, and Nietzsche show the result of the Christian principles that Hegel identifies in a clearer light. By unleashing individual subjectivity, Christianity becomes, in essence, a religion that ultimately undoes itself. Insofar as humans are free and equal, Strauss's argument suggests, there can be no external limits placed on their behavior and categories such as good and evil are rendered meaningless.

Hegel, however, offers an alternative perspective. Spirit, as explicated by Hegel, is free by its nature, and its unfolding in the natural world makes possible a radical equality wherein the finitude of human nature might be made commensurate with the infinite. Freedom and equality, rather than detracting from the objectivity of truth and the possibility of human excellence, are instead the means to, and indeed elements of, the absolute good that Strauss's philosophers sought.

In making this argument, we seek to show not that modernity necessitates Christianity, and we should all thereby be Christian, but rather that Christianity as the representational form of the concept of absolute religion, as Hegel understood it, necessitates modernity, thereby underlining modern ethical life even if, as citizens, we do not consciously take it up as our end. In elaborating upon Hegel's philosophic exposition of the Christian argument, we further seek to demonstrate that many of the objections that Strauss raises against Hegel's philosophy can be answered if one understands this foundation. First, however, it is necessary to clarify Strauss's opposition to Hegel's argument.

STRAUSS AND RELIGION

Faith or Reason

In a number of places, but most clearly in his essay, "Progress or Return," Strauss argues that either philosophy, as understood in the ancient sense, or theology, is required if the modern world is to overcome what he believes is its current crisis. By asserting the existence of a divine and immutable order, both philosophy and theology provide human beings with an intellectual and moral foundation to govern their actions. As Strauss says, the biblical community "has been assigned a place; righteousness in obedience to the divinely established order, just as in classical thought justice is compliance with the natural order; to the recognition of elusive chance corresponds the recognition of inscrutable providence."[8] Importantly, Strauss holds that a life of faith is a positive option for humans, and he argues against those who attempt to logically demonstrate the non-rational nature of this choice.

Yet, he also says that no one can be a citizen of both Athens and Jerusalem, for "No one can be both a philosopher and a theologian nor, for that matter, some possibility of both."[9] The difficulty, according to Strauss, is at the same time philosophical and ethical. Philosophically, Strauss argues, faith and reason are irreconcilable. Religious belief requires unquestioned obedience to inscrutable first principles. In another essay Strauss says, "an omnipotent God who is in principle perfectly knowable to man is in a way subject to man, insofar as knowledge is in a way power. Therefore, a truly omnipotent God must be a mysterious God."[10] The most important things must just be *believed*. The true philosopher, alternatively, can never leave anything unquestioned, and so could not be satisfied by articles of faith. Having reached the limits of his natural knowledge, a philosopher would then hold the Socratic ground of only knowing that he does not know. He would not take as true tenets of belief that which could neither be rationally demonstrated nor understood.[11]

In addition, Strauss argues that the Bible and ancient philosophy have different and even opposing ethical stances. The magnanimous individual, a virtuous person who knows his own worth and is confident that his achievements are the work of his efforts, serves for the Greeks as the highest ethical human type.[12] The biblical suppliant, alternatively, is aware of both his insufficiency and guilt. He subsequently recognizes his absolute dependence on God's inscrutable mercy as the sole cause of any possible goodness in him.[13] A pagan Greek is conscious that he is honorable; an adherent of biblical religion views humility as the appropriate ethical stance.

Describing Greek morality as "heartless" in comparison to its biblical counterpart, Strauss argues that the Greeks did not recognize the value of the biblical virtues, and perceived them as detrimental to the best human life.[14] Biblical morality depends on recognition of one's fault and guilt. Knowing oneself as guilty is to understand oneself as having committed a crime and therefore as prone to error and weakness.[15] The potentially magnanimous person might thereby be caught in a prison of self-doubt if not self-hate, and, not recognizing his worth, would be unable to do the great things that he is capable of doing.[16] According to Strauss, the ethics of the Bible seem to directly oppose the ethical life promoted by ancient philosophers. Interestingly, this is also the argument made by Nietzsche, albeit somewhat more hyperbolically.[17]

This picture is further complicated when one notes that neither Plato nor Aristotle believed the ethical life to be the best life, but instead, crowned the contemplative life of philosophers with the highest honor. Strauss perceives this to be in direct contrast to the prominence of ethics in the Bible for, he argues, the life of contemplation ultimately lessens the claims of ethics.

As we saw in the previous chapter, Strauss says that philosophy is antithetical to human community or the place of one's ethical activity.[18] Living in a community, while necessary for the sake of one's physical well-being, is at the same time a distraction from the proper object of thought. Communal life requires that we pay attention to the people who surround us. Ensuring that the demands of one's political community, friends, family and physical self are met leaves little, if any, time to contemplate the nature of Being. If true, the real philosopher must strive to distance himself as far as possible from these worries and, thus, from the life of practical virtue, which, by its nature, is concerned with human beings as perishable creatures in contingent situations.[19] Tanquay explains, "the theoretical and contemplative attitude is in fact a fundamental trans-social, transpolitical, and we would dare say in accord with the spirit of Strauss, a trans-moral attitude. The gaze with which the philosopher looks at the world is a gaze indifferent to the distinction between the beautiful and the ugly, good and evil."[20]

Readers of Plato and Aristotle will note how idiosyncratic an interpretation this is of ancient philosophy, particularly in light of Plato's portrayal of Socrates as continuously interested in questions of morality and Aristotle's significant works on ethics. It is also important to note that Strauss argues that the philosopher, desiring the good, desires its manifestation in the world around him. He encourages its representation, in the form of virtue, in the souls that he deems to be fertile ground for its development. The philosopher seeks to create "good" people, as a way to further reflect on the nature of the Good, if only in a partial and contingent form.[21] Moreover, as we have seen, Strauss understood the second best life to be that of the gentleman, a person who strove to live a life of ethical virtue. As life in the *polis* is necessary, the rule of gentlemen is preferable to any of the alternatives. Hence, Strauss does not deny the importance of ethics. He does argue, however, that ancient philosophy necessarily has only a secondary interest in ethics.

Unlike ancient Greek philosophy, Strauss says that biblical faith raises to preeminence the ethical. Starting from a point of subservient obedience, the faithful should not be concerned about the life of the mind; they must do as they are told. Strauss points to the story of the Garden of Eden and the forbidden fruit that, if eaten, would grant knowledge of good and evil. Interpreting these passages, Strauss concludes, "Man is not meant to be a theoretical, a knowing, a contemplating being; man is meant to live in childlike obedience."[22] Once this first law is broken and the metaphorical fruit has been eaten, the pursuit of knowledge and understanding becomes an unfortunate but necessary activity. Even then, however, knowledge is sought and directed to the service of God. Thrown out of the natural paradise, humans are forced to labor and must find the path back to righteousness. The pursuit of knowledge in this account is a necessary evil.

Further, Strauss argues that, in contrast to the philosopher, a faithful person's ethical activity is a necessary and direct result of his beliefs. One's faith is demonstrated by recognizing guilt, and in consequent acts of repentance. Faith in divine mercy brings with it necessary and new ethical virtues, such as charity.[23] While the Greek philosopher is always aware that he does not know, and his prudence dictates caution, if not inactivity when attempting to put "theory" into practice, if one has faith, one will be certain. While particular circumstances may not always dictate a clear line of activity, for the faithful the larger end, or the good that one intends to secure, will always be apparent. Knowing the higher command, the faithful direct their hearts in the pursuit of this end.[24] Finally, faith in a merciful God results in forgiveness. Whatever he has done, trusting in God's mercy, the faithful person is righteous. There is no reason to hesitate in action, for it is the purity of one's heart that is important.[25] All of these things lead to what Strauss describes as the "majesty of moral demands" for the faithful.[26]

It is clear to those who have read Strauss, that of the two cities, Athens and Jerusalem, he has chosen Athens. This is particularly evident in his interpretative lecture on *Genesis*. Strauss distinguishes between how one should read the Bible versus how one should read works written by human authors in a similar tone to Machiavelli.[27] Other books, Strauss argues, should be approached with the intent to question and analyze what is written so as to reveal the author's intent while, perhaps, going beyond his thought to understanding the theme as a whole. The Bible, however, being the work of God, "has to be read in a spirit of pious submission, of reverent hearing."[28] And yet, when Strauss proceeds to read *Genesis*, he does so with the disclaimer that, as a scholar and even as a man of science, he can neither prove nor disprove the existence of an omnipotent God and thus, "[is] reduced to a state of doubt in regard to the most important question. We have no choice but to approach the Bible in this state of doubt."[29] Like other works, scholars must seek to *understand* the Bible, as opposed to having faith in the literal meaning of its words. One might note how Strauss formulates this argument. It is in "his capacity as a scholar," that Strauss reads the Bible, putting aside the possibility that as a faithful Jew, he might approach the Bible differently. Yet, given what he says is the incompatibility of a life of faith with a life of reason, there would seem to be a tension that he believes the human mind cannot successfully overcome. Elsewhere, Strauss says, "By saying that we wish to hear first and then to act to decide, we have already decided in favor of Athens against Jerusalem."[30]

Moreover, as a result of the type of philosophy Strauss pursues, the unbridgeable chasm that he envisions between the things of philosophy and the things of faith widens; Strauss's understanding of the relationship between the metaphysical and physical lends itself to a particularly anti-metaphysical form of philosophy. Strauss argues that human knowledge begins in the experience of the phenomenal world.[31] By a process of induction the individual seeks to draw universal conclusions. The type of universal truth, however, that a person can thereby understand is limited to what is universally true of the "given whole." Strauss describes what can be known: "the whole which is permanently given, as permanently as are human beings, the whole which is held together and constituted by the vault of heaven and earth and everything that is within heaven and earth and between heaven and earth."[32] In other words, the philosopher seeks knowledge of the natural order and the "universal" principles that can be derived from this. Rather ironically then, given Strauss's criticism of modern philosophers whose arguments do not allow for knowledge or even the existence of a metaphysical first principle, Strauss's own philosophy is similarly limited.

While Strauss indicates that such a cosmology is insufficient for the purposes of wisdom, pointing out that Plato knew that one had to move beyond the heavenly to a super-heavenly place, it is also apparent that Strauss did not think that such a transcendent position could be achieved.[33] He thereby attributes to Aristotle the understanding that the principles that direct our political and practical lives are distinct from those principles that are purely theoretical.[34] Ethical life does not depend on any metaphysical foundations. Instead, humans discern their proper end by investigating human nature and determining which activities will result in human happiness. Strauss limits human knowledge to the physical and mutable realm of nature, leading Rosen to note that in Strauss's thought, "On the central point . . . there seems to be little difference between the ancients and the moderns."[35]

This, however, is a strange argument for Strauss to make about Aristotle. Practical wisdom, Aristotle argues, is knowledge about contingent and variable things. Insofar as human beings partake in the realm of contingency, practical wisdom includes understanding the best life for a human being.[36] Theoretical wisdom, alternatively, concerns itself with the eternal and immutable. The best human life will overcome these apparent divisions in knowledge, for humans are not merely contingent, but also partake of the divine via their rational souls.[37] Humans are both particular and objective beings, and these two elements are dialectically involved in human happiness. While Aristotle would agree with Strauss that the best life is one of contemplation and an ethical life is only second best, he does not see these two lives as unrelated.[38] Aristotle indicates that the purpose of ethical virtue, and of prudence, is to prepare and enable a life of wisdom and understanding.[39] The prudent person must know his proper end—the life of contemplation—and achieve a kind of ethical life that will foster this development.[40] Further, through the practice of good acts, Aristotle says we come to understand and desire the good; and the better we understand the nature of the good, the more able and willing we are to direct ourselves to the particular goods that are the objects of ethics.[41] Finally, in the *Metaphysics,* a text on which Strauss does not comment, Aristotle tells us that knowledge of the Absolute, in and of itself, is the grounds for all other knowledge.[42]

According to Aristotle, the particular and practical happiness of human beings depends in part on their seeking theoretical wisdom. Strauss implies the necessary relationship between practical wisdom and theoretical wisdom when he says that we can philosophically derive an account of the divine from our experience of the most perfect human—the wise man. By familiarizing ourselves with the best natures amongst us, we can understand something about the nature of the good.[43] There is apparently no necessary division between theoretical wisdom and practical understanding and, in fact, in human understanding. The two seem necessarily linked. As Strauss says, human beings begin their investigation of the metaphysical through their physical experience, enhancing and, perhaps, completing their practical and physical lives through this metaphysical knowledge.

Despite this, Strauss still posits an essential opposition between eternal metaphysical truths and the contingency of the physical world. This may explain why Strauss argues that Plato's doctrine of the forms is meant ironically rather than assertively.[44] Images, ultimately, can never tell us about what truly is.[45] Of Hegel, Strauss writes, "Reason has reached its perfection in . . . [his] system; the essential limitations of his system show the essential limitations of reason. . . . Reason knows only of subjects and objects, but surely the living God is infinitely more than a subject and can never be an object, something at which one can look in detachment or indifference."[46] It is on these grounds that Strauss says, "philosophy in the original meaning of the term is nothing but knowledge of one's ignorance."[47] As such, Strauss questions any claims made about metaphysics, and he says of political science, his chosen field, "social science demands from us . . . to start from the solid, if low facts and to remain as much as possible on the ground. No flights of fancy, no science fiction, no metaphysics will enter. That is clear."[48] Through experience, reasoning, and understanding we speculate about the metaphysical by means of our relationship to the physical, but this knowledge will presumably always be tinged with the particularity that defines the natural world.

Despite Strauss's claim that the highest life is the philosophic life, the life that seeks the highest knowledge of the highest of things, his own focus is not theology, metaphysics, or ontology, but rather political philosophy, the study of the best human life. Meier says, "The question that Strauss seeks to answer with his historical interpretation explicitly reads 'what is political philosophy?' and not 'what is metaphysics?'"[49] As such, Strauss seems much more akin to the modern account that he critiques. Therefore, Rosen notes, "Strauss's critique of modernity although at its surface is political, takes us directly to the depths and thus not to politics but to what used to be called metaphysics and is now known as ontology. . . . What makes Strauss difficult to understand is his failure to carry through his argument at its own proper level."[50] For Strauss, any account that asserts a particular understanding of metaphysics is true, as opposed to a mere hypothesis, which can only be a doctrine of faith, not an act of philosophy.

Christianity as Subjectivity

As we shall see, Strauss's account of the irreconcilability of faith and reason immediately puts him at odds with Hegel's understanding. However, further complicating Strauss's approach to Hegel is that Strauss's account of Biblical faith, naturally enough, focuses predominantly on the Old Testament and the Jewish faith, and not Christianity.[51] One might attribute this focus to Strauss's religious heritage and early academic influence. For as Strauss says:

> it is impossible to get rid of one's past. It is necessary to accept one's past. That means that out of this undeniable necessity one must make a virtue. The virtue in question is fidelity, loyalty, piety in the Latin sense of the term *pietas*. The necessity of taking this step appears from the disgraceful character of the only alternative, of denying one's origin, past, or heritage.[52]

As admirable as this statement is, for someone who has chosen the philosophic alternative rather than numbering himself among the faithful, it is peculiar that, seeking to understand what is true regardless of its origin, Strauss does not spend more time explicitly understanding Christian philosophy. While Strauss wrote commentaries on the book of *Genesis* and Maimonides, for instance, he has no corresponding commentaries on

John's Gospel or Aquinas. Needless to say, no one can be expected to investigate in a detailed manner all avenues of potential interest. Yet the range of Strauss's scholarship is impressively broad, extending from the ancient world to the modern. As a result, the lack of any extended commentary on the Christian medieval period is conspicuous in its absence.

For instance, when Strauss does turn his attention to Marsilius of Padua, an explicitly Christian, albeit heterodox, philosopher, he does so on the grounds that Marsilius himself distinguishes between reason that is possible by means of human demonstration, and knowledge that is dependent on revelation and exists as an object of faith. Strauss bifurcates Marsilius's political thought from his theology and studies one without commenting on the other.[53] This Kantian reading of Marsilius fits neatly with Strauss's reduction of reason's scope. In moving directly from Maimonides to Marsilius, Strauss simply avoids any substantial engagement with Aquinas's medieval synthesis of faith and reason.

This is further complicated by Strauss's claim that Christianity is dependent on philosophy in a way that Judaism is not. He explains, "For the Jew and the Moslem, religion is primarily not as it is for the Christian, a faith formulated in dogmas, but a law, a code of divine origin." And while laws are meant to be obeyed, dogmas must, at least in part, be understood. "Hence the status of philosophy is, as a matter of principle, much more precarious in the Islamic-Jewish world than it is in the Christian world. No one could become a competent Christian theologian without having studied at least a sizeable part of philosophy; philosophy was an integral part of the officially authorized and even required training."[54] Strauss goes on to note the significant difference in the opening problems of Aquinas's and Maimonides's seminal works. While Aquinas tests the necessity of revelation in the court of reason, Maimonides tests the possibility of philosophy in the court of traditional Jewish law.[55] And yet these points do not ultimately make Christian thought truly philosophic. Instead, Strauss argues that philosophy is not adequately free in Christian regimes and, as such, cannot be taken to its true end.

According to Strauss, the official place of philosophy in the Christian order meant all philosophic accounts that were allowed to flourish, at least in its medieval life, had to survive official scrutiny. The church welcomed philosophy as a means for more fully controlling and regulating the development of thought. Alternatively, Strauss tells us, inasmuch as philosophy had to be covertly conducted in medieval Jewish and Muslim worlds, proponents of the life of wisdom became fluent in finding private ways of living this life. Ironically then, Strauss argues that the prohibition against philosophy for Jews made it much more likely that real philosophy could flourish.[56] This argument of course leaves aside the very real, if not Straussian, possibility that Christian medieval philosophers would be as aware as Strauss of the effect of the Church's authority on their works and the possibility that, like their Jewish and Muslim counterparts, they found ways around this. In a more explicitly critical vein, in making the argument that the past is preferable to future progress, Strauss wonders, "But does the hope for redemption—the expectation of the Messiah—not assign a much higher place to the future than to the past, however venerable?" And he responds, "This is not unqualifiedly true. According to the most accepted view, the Messiah is inferior to Moses."[57]

A partial, but necessarily incomplete, explanation of Strauss's argument in this respect seems to lie in the philosophic principles that animate certain interpretations of Christianity, specifically the emphasis on history and subjectivity that Hegel's interpretation reveals.[58] Batnitzky explains, "Strauss was not indifferent to the content of revelation, and certainly not to the difference between Jewish and Christian notions of revelation. In fact, Strauss strongly criticizes what he regards as a particularly Christian view of revelation . . . suggest[ing] that modernity's intellectual ills stem from the legacy of Christian theology."[59] Strauss says:

> Modernity was understood from the beginning in contradistinction from antiquity; modernity could therefore include the medieval world. The difference between the modern and the medieval on the one hand, and antiquity on the other, was reinterpreted around eighteen hundred as the difference between the romantic and the classic.[60]

The romantic position, into which Strauss collapses Christianity, is in many ways the very essence of what he finds distasteful about modernity. To be clear, our argument is not concerned with whether Strauss (or anyone else) should accept the Christian religion. Rather, we are arguing that Strauss ignores, for whatever reason, an account of the biblical tradition that is challenging to his philosophical position.

Romanticism, Strauss says, highlights particular and subjective experiences, focusing on an individual's apprehension of and reactions to the world rather than on what should be objectively understood and subsequently responded to. Strauss uses Goethe's *Faust* as the epitome of the romantic Christian perspective. That God calls Faust good despite the fact that he is not virtuous indicates to Strauss a clear break with the ancient Greek and presumably Jewish account of morality in favor of a morality that no longer depends on one's objective actions, but rather on the subjective content of one's heart. It matters not what Faust has done or not done, what matters is merely his intentions.[61] Christianity, and the modern world more broadly, err in highlighting human subjectivity, thereby making objective judgments on truth and activity irrelevant and impossible.

When describing the nature of the philosophic endeavor, Strauss notes that contingent and historical matters are not an appropriate focus. Particular realities in the finite world cannot, according to Strauss, speak clearly enough to the universal truths that are at the heart of philosophic striving. Insofar as revelation and the things revealed are understood as particular events occurring in history, they are not the proper scope of philosophy. When Strauss does turn his attention to what must be understood as a philosophic interpretation of *Genesis*, he seeks what is universally true within this account; he seeks to understand its account of the 'whole': "All human thought, even all thought human or divine, which is meant to be understood by human beings willy nilly begins with this whole, the permanently given whole which we all know and which men always know."[62] While Strauss understands the whole as referring to the natural cosmos, in striving even to understand it, the philosopher must bypass particular and contingent events, specifically those that depart from the universal trends that this whole demonstrates.

Alternatively, Christianity focuses on particular and historical events, specifically the life of Christ, and the Christian faith depends upon adherents taking this particular historical fact seriously. That God appears in history indicates that absolute truth or even philosophy is not incompatible with or unconnected to time and history. This eventually results in the radical historicism that Strauss understands as undermining the possibility of theology and the entire philosophic project. He notes, "Historicism emerged in the nineteenth century under the protection of the belief that knowledge or at least divination of the eternal is possible. But it gradually undermined the belief which had sheltered it in its infancy."[63] According to Strauss, radical historicism asserts that all actions are determined by the particular context of their historical moment and cannot be understood except within this context. The possibility of knowledge is thereby limited to particular moments in time and one cannot transcend the context of a historical moment to objectively assess it in light of a more complete account. Radical historicism finds its roots in Christianity, and ironically becomes the catalyst behind Christianity's downfall.

Hegel's acceptance of historicism, although much less radical in nature than what Strauss describes, at least partially explains Strauss's argument that Hegel's philosophy is purely secular in nature. Indeed, it seems that Strauss understands Hegel as subjecting even God to the historical process. Unlike Aquinas, who Strauss uses as the comparator, Hegel argues that God is bound by necessity to create for the fulfillment of his self-consciousness.[64] To be in and for himself, God must become an object for his own contemplation and he accomplishes this through the creation of the world. As such, Strauss argues, even God is not perfectly free or absolute. Correspondingly, in contrast to Aristotle's unmoved mover, Strauss argues that Hegel's God is "a moving mover." By moving, God is at the same time moved or, at the very least, not eternal or all knowing.[65] The result of this reading for Strauss leads him to admit, although not without reservation, that Hegel reduces the divine to the human. On the question of whether Hegel's philosophy admits of a transcendent first principle, Strauss, in his lectures, notes that, "Hegel is extremely ambiguous." Despite this ambiguity, Strauss concludes, "it is doubtful whether Hegel did not mean that consciousness of freedom is achieved only in man, but since man is part of this whole order, this more than human order, you can say, of course, that this is God in man."[66] As a result of this understanding of Hegel's thought, Strauss writes, "According to a very common notion, modernity is secularized biblical faith: the other worldly biblical faith has become radically this worldly. Most simply: not to hope for life in heaven but to establish heaven on earth by purely human means."[67]

This reduction of Hegel's understanding of Spirit to a secular form of philosophy leads Strauss to assert that the only absolute truth that exists for Hegel is the contingency of human life. In so doing, Hegel, Strauss suggests, undermines his argument. Strauss understands that Hegel projects an account of freedom as ultimately rational and moral. However, by reducing the divine to the human, Hegel denies the possibility of any objective good governing the process of human development. As a result, Strauss says, "Hegel continued, and in a certain sense, radicalized the modern tradition that emancipated the passions." And, "Hegel's teaching is more sophisticated than Hobbes', but it is as much a construction as the latter. Both doctrines construct human society by starting from the untrue assumption that man as man is thinkable as a being that lacks awareness of sacred restraints or as a being that is guided by nothing but a desire for recognition."[68] Ultimately, Hegel, just as much as Hobbes, Strauss argues, reduces human ethics such that appetite is the only arbiter of good and bad. Fixing his attention on the moment of the conflict between the consciousness of master and slave, Strauss argues that Hegel, like Hobbes, perceives human beings in their most natural state without any knowledge of the divine.[69] However, Strauss does not follow Hegel's account of the development of human consciousness from this initial state to what Hegel describes as self-consciousness, a state that requires an understanding of the nature of Spirit and its relationship to human life.[70] Instead, Strauss perceives the Hegelian state of self-consciousness to begin and end with human passions, ungoverned by any eternal principles.

Although Tanquay argues that any attempt, such as Hegel's, to synthesize Christianity with modernity, can only occur by "denaturing the theological concepts proper to Revelation . . . [preparing] the way for the final victory of the radical Enlightenment, that is of atheism," Strauss's position appears less nuanced. [71] For Strauss, it seems that Christianity is the root of modernity and thus, in some significant way, serves as the primary cause for his dissatisfaction with the modern world. Hegel also recognizes the relationship between Christianity and modernity; unlike Strauss, however, Hegel perceives the development of modernity from and in conformity with its Christian roots as an indication of humanity discovering its true potential.

HEGEL AND RELIGION

Faith and Reason

Hegel's philosophic endeavor is in direct opposition to Strauss's philosophic inclinations. As Strauss tells us, Hegel believed that "Christianity is the true or absolute religion . . . [and that] Christianity consists in its reconciliation with the world."[72] Leaving aside momentarily whether this is an accurate account of what Hegel thought, or true of the Christian position, such a claim, from Strauss's perspective, is implausible, if not impossible. The immutability of a transcendent God is necessarily in tension, if not in opposition, to the natural world. Finally rejecting the idea of an infinite god who makes himself commensurate with the finite, Strauss suggests instead that Hegel's philosophy raises the human world to a level where the divine is no longer a required category.

In leaving Hegel's exposition of Christianity unattended, Strauss strips Hegel's thought of its proper foundation. Interestingly, Strauss begins his lectures on Hegel's *Philosophy of History* explaining why he has chosen to read these rather than *The Philosophy of Right*, a text that Hegel consciously wrote for publication, saying that in addition to being written in a fashion that is easier to comprehend, Hegel's account of history is foundational to understanding his political thought.[73] While this is certainly true, Hegel's account of history is itself founded on Hegel's understanding that the divine reveals itself historically, as demonstrated in his philosophic exposition of the Christian religion. As such, a surer place to begin would be perhaps in Hegel's *Encyclopedia* or, attending to Strauss's point that Hegel's lecture style is more accessible than his writing style, his *Lectures on the Philosophy of Religion*. As a result of not investigating Hegel's account of Christianity more fulsomely, Strauss's criticisms of Hegel are, in large part, unfounded. Further, we believe this dismissal accounts for a more pessimistic view about the prospects for modernity. In the following sections, we will explore Hegel's presentation of Christianity and respond more directly to Strauss's criticisms. In making our response we have predominantly, but not exclusively, focused on Hegel's *Lectures on the Philosophy of Religion* from 1827. Hegel lectures four different times on the philosophy of religion: 1821, 1824, 1827, and 1831. From 1821, there exists a draft form, but not the final manuscript, of Hegel's lecture notes. From 1824 and 1827, several students' lecture notes have been retained, compared and edited. No complete set of notes from 1831 seems to have survived. As a result, the 1827 lectures are representative of the most complete version of Hegel's working out of his thoughts on the philosophy of religion. However, recognizing that Hegel would be responding to different questions or themes each time he lectured, we have also made extensive use of the other lectures when it seemed warranted.[74]

While Hegel's account of Spirit and its relationship to human thought and activity pervades all of his works, most notably the *Logic* and the *Phenomenology of Spirit, The Lectures on the Philosophy of Religion* seem most appropriate in this context for several reason. First, Hegel turned his attention to formulating his thought about the philosophy of religion within the last decade of his life. While he did not live to see them published, they speak to what must have been a particular interest in his mature thought.[75] Jaeschke convincingly explains why Hegel's lectures on the philosophy religion should be examined with a good deal of confidence—they are reflective of Hegel's fullest thought on the subject. For, unlike the section on religion in the *Phenomenology of Spirit*, which is published early in Hegel's career, his lectures on the philosophy of religion reflect his mature thought. Moreover, while the text of the *Encyclopedia* is from the same period, its treatment of religion is much briefer, and encompassed by the much longer exposition from the lectures.[76] Furthermore, in the context of a response to Strauss, the lectures most explicitly present the position that is the focus of several of Strauss's concerns, particularly the nature of the relationship of faith to reason, and the way in which Hegel understands modern society as secular in nature. We will begin with Hegel's account of the proper relationship of faith and reason.

Contrary to Strauss's argument, and in response to Kant's *Critique*, Hegel insists that there is no irreconcilable tension between faith and reason, and that these two kinds of knowledge are ultimately the same, sharing a common end: "it must be said that the content of philosophy, its need and interest, is wholly in common with that of religion. The object of religion, like that of philosophy, is the eternal truth, God and nothing but God and the explication of God."[77] While religion appears in a different guise than philosophy, its true nature unfolds in a distinct and yet parallel way, achieving the same purpose.

In fact, revelation, Hegel tells us, is the nature of Spirit as well as the nature of truth. Divine self-consciousness necessitates that it is both in and for itself, or both subject and object, contrary to Strauss's assertion that it can be neither. The revelation of the created order, the revelation of the Bible, and the revelation of Christ are all parts of the logical unfolding of the divine nature or the ways by which Spirit becomes an object for its own contemplation:

> What God reveals in this way is that he *is* manifestation. . . . It is his nature and his concept eternally to make these distinctions and at the same time take them back into himself, and thereby to be present to himself. The content that becomes manifest is what is revealed, namely, that God is for an *other*, but also eternally for *himself*."[78]

By means of revelation, Spirit fulfills its nature and demonstrates the full potentiality of human nature as well. By means of revelation, the absolute instructs that it is to be known and places an obligation on human beings to achieve this knowledge. As Hegel remarks, "God wishes no narrow hearted souls or empty heads for his children."[79] According to Hegel, the nature of Spirit is reason. Understanding the actualization of its nature is the fullest possible epistemology. Moreover, the actualization of reason is the very process through which human understanding occurs. As this relates directly to Kojève's account of the desire for recognition, it is useful to examine this argument more closely.

Spirit, according to Hegel, is absolute truth. However, the nature of truth is such that it must be both in and for itself. In other words, subjective certainty is not sufficient for a full understanding of what is; in addition, what is known subjectively must also be objectively true. For this reason, Hegel says, "Spirit *knows itself*. It involves an appreciation of its own nature, as also an energy enabling it to realize itself; to make itself *actually* that which it is *potentially*" and "it follows that God can be known or cognized, for it is God's nature to reveal himself, to be manifest."[80] The nature of the absolute as truth results in its objective manifestation in the created order and, ultimately, in revelation.

Spirit thereby makes its nature an object for its own understanding. In so doing, it becomes its own antithesis; the uncreated becomes created and the infinite becomes finite. Epistemologically this occurs because recognizing the true nature of something requires seeing it in relationship to what it is not. These two moments are then sublated. The initial understanding one had is deepened as the knowledge of that truth's limits and boundaries, now newly defined, become an integral part of what is understood. Spirit, as absolute and universal, actualizes the fullness of its nature by making itself an object by means of the created, natural world.[81] Through its creation of and therefore reconciliation with the world, the differences between the infinite and the finite, the objective and the subjective, are sublated and the truth of each is revealed.

A particular person comes to consciousness of himself through the process of recognition. In the process of recognition, the individual knows himself as both a universal being, by means of the common traits, particularly rationality, that he shares with others, and as a subjective being by means of those elements of his nature that are distinct from others. Correspondingly, the absolute nature of Spirit becomes an object for its consciousness in the created order. It knows itself as infinite and absolute in contrast to the finite and limited being of nature, but it also knows itself as universal truth by means of its commonality with human consciousness. While the processes of nature may be in accord with reason, they are not rational in and of themselves and cannot reflect the full truth of divine self-consciousness. Self-consciousness is only objective and complete when *freely* taken up by other rational beings, by human beings who are potentially self-conscious themselves. Hegel writes, "God as spirit is this process, whose moments have themselves the shape of complete reality and thereby of finite self-consciousness. . . . God must be for himself as the whole of revelation; only thus is he revealed. This history of his must be an object for him, but in *its own* objectivity and truth."[82] In the freely achieved self-consciousness of people, Spirit becomes truth not merely in itself, but also for itself. This is the nature of truth and the nature of Spirit, for "this revealing or self-manifesting belongs to the essence of spirit itself. *A spirit that is not revelatory is not spirit.*"[83] In manifesting itself, Spirit reveals its full nature and creates other thinking beings that ultimately have the capacity to exhibit what is subjectively certain about the absolute in an external and objective way.[84]

Interpreting the representational language that humans are made in God's image, Hegel understands people as participating in the nature and activity of Spirit, fulfilling both it and themselves in the development of self-consciousness. The actualization of human reason and self-consciousness proceeds by means of the same logic as the actualization of Spirit.[85] As the above example indicates, gaining a certain understanding of oneself, or becoming an object for one's subjective apprehension, requires that another free and rational being reflect this same understanding.[86] The completion of one's knowledge depends on a community with at least one other source of reflection who both knows what is sought and confirms what is understood as, indeed, being true. In agreement with Kojève, at least on this point, Hegel writes, "[self-consciousness] would have truth only if its own being-for-self had confronted it as an independent object. Or, what is the same thing, if the object had presented itself as this pure self-certainty."[87] In each of his arguments, Hegel describes how, in the various aspects of human life, we achieve and make manifest the nature of Spirit. The *Phenomenology* describes this process philosophically, while the *Aesthetics* takes it up in the works of human art, and *Elements of the Philosophy of Right* describes the process as political development. In the *Lectures on the Philosophy of Religion* Hegel describes how this process is effected through religious life.

According to Hegel, religion begins in immediacy in intuition or feeling: "My intuiting and feeling, and all such sensible knowledge, is wholly immediate, unmediated—there is no ground for it. Here belief in general has the meaning of 'immediate certainty'."[88] When people concentrate on their feelings, the object of their concentration is themselves and themselves in a particular and wholly subjective sense.[89] Antigone, a favorite example of Hegel's, says that one cannot know where the laws of the gods have come from. These laws, as opposed to human laws, are immediately intuited rather than known or understood.[90] The divine laws exist for Antigone insofar as she can sense their presence. By responding to what she senses, she becomes righteous and indignant. Antigone's subjective feelings are the only proof she requires that she is acting correctly. Although Antigone seeks to act in accordance with what is most objectively and universally true, her actions are entirely in response to her subjective experience, and, in the end, she is isolated and alone.[91] On these grounds, it is perhaps easy to conclude, along with Strauss, that faith is in opposition to the rational process of philosophy. After all, by the end of *Antigone*, Creon has at least ceded the rational place of the family and its gods, while Antigone fails to recognize the value of the state.[92]

Hegel, however, argues that while faith might begin with a sense of immediacy, this is only one moment of a much longer journey. When discussing the immediacy of religious feeling, Hegel notes that feelings are in response to things and they can be appropriate or inappropriate, right or wrong. Hegel asks, "Is then something true or legitimate because it is in my feeling? Is feeling the verification, or must the content be just, true, or ethical in and for itself?" He concludes, "If feeling is the justifying element, then the distinction between good and evil comes to naught, for evil with all its shadings and qualifications is in feeling just as much as the good."[93] Even though Hegel argues that religious belief begins in the immediate apprehension of the divine, he understands that this is neither its final nor most complete moment. Immediacy and feeling must proceed to mediation and thought, or understanding, for "one's feelings or one's heart must be purified or cultivated."[94] Hegel makes the distinction that while one may be immediately certain of something, having conviction or being convinced requires demonstration.[95] And even further, he argues that immediate apprehension or feeling is ultimately nonsensical inasmuch as all of one's apprehensions are caused and mediated by something else.[96] Put another way, insofar as one is distinct from Spirit, the apprehension one might have that there is a god must come from somewhere; it is not immediately identical to one's own existence. And while these feelings may be identical with some moment in one's soul, they must be aroused by or mediated by something else.

As the nature of Spirit is self-consciousness this too is the proper nature of human beings.[97] To rest satisfied in the awareness of the absolute as an immediate intuition, when such immediacy is an illusion, is to lack awareness of both the self and its end. Human nature, and that of the absolute, both demand that humans rise above this misapprehension and come to a fuller awareness of truth. According to Hegel, not only is faith not in opposition to reason, but it requires reason for completion.[98] Williamson writes, "a mere unthinking faith is not truly a faith at all . . . [it] is merely a 'blind' faith that is really dehumanizing."[99] For this reason, Hegel is able to resuscitate, albeit in changed form, the traditional proofs that had been dismissed by Kant for the existence of God.

Helpfully, Catherine and Michael Zuckert further clarify Strauss's critique of Hegel on this point, explaining that had a system of knowledge been truly completed, then the tension between faith and reason should have disappeared.[100] The remaining conflict indicates to Strauss that such a system of knowledge does not exist. And, as stated earlier, Strauss further argues the omnipotence of the divine has its mystery as a necessary consequence.[101]

Hegel disputes both of these arguments. He stresses that the availability of the truth does not necessarily coincide with one's choosing to know it.[102] Unlike the ancient account, wherein it is argued that if we truly know the good then we will pursue it, the Christian account argues that we can absolutely know what is good and choose to will otherwise.[103] Hence, Paul writes, "For the good that I would I do not: but the evil which I would not, that I do."[104] And Augustine, perceiving the truth of Christian position, is nonetheless able to pray, "Grant me chastity and continence, but not yet."[105] While Hegel says that Christianity places an absolute responsibility on human beings to understand their true end, he is not naïve in his belief that all humans will fulfill this requirement. For as he says, "In affirming . . . that the Universal Reason *does* realize itself, we have indeed nothing to do with the individual empirically regarded. That admits of degrees of better and worse, since here chance and specialty have received authority from the Idea to exercise their monstrous power."[106] That Hegel did not think that all people would raise themselves from representation to a philosophic cognition of Spirit does not detract from his argument that this is the fullest form of religious belief, in the same way that Strauss's understanding that we will not all be philosophers does not detract from his account that this is still the happiest human life. What this means for Hegel's account of political and ethical lives will be discussed later.

In addition, Hegel opposes the argument that the nature of Spirit necessitates its mystery. The actualization of Spirit requires the self-conscious reflection of its being in others; Spirit must be both in and for itself. Knowledge of Spirit is necessitated by the nature of truth.[107] Nor is it sufficient, according to Hegel, to know what God commands and respond with blind obedience without seeking to understand the nature of these commands: "It is not simply valid for us externally because it *is* so; rather it is also valid for us internally, it is rationally valid as something essential."[108] Following the spirit of the law requires that the law be internally understood rather than merely externally promulgated. In direct response to Strauss's claim that the divine nature must be mysterious, Hegel says, "Among the Athenians the death penalty was exacted if one did not allow another person to light his lamp from one's own, for one lost nothing by doing so. In the same way God loses nothing when he communicates himself."[109] While Hegel concedes that the absolute nature of Spirit may not be fully knowable to humans in their finitude, it is incumbent upon the faithful to seek as complete a knowledge as is possible so that they might better know and achieve self-consciousness.

Seeking knowledge, Adam and Eve become philosophers and, as a result, are thrown out of the garden. Strauss says, "What to the classical philosophers appeared as the perfection of man's nature is described by the Bible as the product of man's disobedience."[110] However, the account of Christianity, as taken up by Hegel, is that the perfect innocence that defines the original state of human beings is insufficient to their true natures as free and rational creatures.[111] The completion of human nature requires the fall as humans must know all of the possibilities before them, the good as well as the bad, and then freely make their choice. Becoming philosophers and being thrown out of the garden are not to be perceived negatively—they are moments in the process of human completion. Hegel explains that the development of human consciousness, reflected in the image of eating from the tree of knowledge, is a necessary moment in the fulfillment of human nature: "this first [form of] reflection, according to which the natural is [regarded] as evil, is a situation that ought not to be, i.e., it ought to be sublated—but it is not one that ought not to occur: it has occurred because human being is consciousness."[112] In other words, once human beings achieve the consciousness that differentiates them from animals, they gain an understanding, however rudimentary, of the possibility of an ethical life. With this knowledge, humans necessarily know themselves as finite or "fallen," for the good is universally and eternally true, but humans are conscious of their mortality and natural desires.[113] It is this consciousness that Christianity sublates and overcomes, according to Hegel. Knowing the nature of the good, and its opposite, is what ultimately allows humans to willingly transcend their natures as finite beings.

Ironically, Hegel would argue that Strauss's position, that objects of faith must be accepted and believed rather than understood, dilutes the content of religion and releases the destructive claims of relativism into our ethical lives.[114] Insofar as it is accepted that objects of faith are to be believed rather than understood, religion is left open to the criticisms of the skeptical philosopher, who is turned away at the door for seeking proof on the grounds that such proof is either impossible or inappropriate. Correspondingly, when the faithful are given no persuasive grounds to accept some beliefs rather than others, the freedom of the modern world will, of course, encourage them to take up what speaks most persuasively to *them* as the basis of thought and action.[115] While Strauss derides the attempt to philosophically cognize the nature of God, for Hegel, seeking a scientific understanding is necessary to fulfill one's end as a self-conscious and ethical being.

The Reconciliation of Subjectivity and Objectivity

As noted earlier, a central element of Strauss's critique of Hegel's philosophy rests on Strauss's belief that Hegel secularizes Christianity, reducing the absolute to the human, and transforming any heavenly paradise to a purely earthly garden. In Strauss's reading, by secularizing religion, Hegel ultimately and perhaps unintentionally denies the role of universal and objective truths in guiding a good human life. Instead, one is left to his purely subjective and particular devices and passions. As indicated earlier, Strauss suggests that despite his efforts to transcend Hobbes, Hegel is merely a more sophisticated version. This is also the ground of Strauss's charge that Hegel is a radical historicist.

Strauss's undeveloped account of Hegel's concept of spirit broadly agrees with a strong element in Hegelian scholarship that argues that the actualization of spirit refers only to the development of self-consciousness in human beings, and, as such, does not require any transcendent principle. Proponents of this position argue that Hegel is in greater agreement with Kant than previously allowed. As such, it is argued that Hegel fundamentally agrees with the understanding that human knowledge is limited to experience of the phenomenal world. In this light, progressions in human understanding are understood as in reference to a fuller appreciation of the nature and actualization of the human mind and/or in reference to historical developments in cultures and institutions that rationally respond to previous deficiencies. Despite this general agreement with Strauss, most of these scholars would still disagree with his rendering of Hegel, for although they argue that Hegel denies the presence of a transcendent first principle, they also argue that one can nonetheless find a principle of objectivity within human thought and social activity.[116]

While much of what these scholars have to say about Hegel's account of the development of human understanding and activity is persuasive, we ultimately find this position unconvincing insofar as it denies the fullness of Hegel's thought. Certainly much, if not the largest part, of Hegel's project is to detail the progression of human thought. At the same time, however, it is difficult to ignore the strength of Hegel's statements around the presence of an objective Spirit that is clearly related to human development, but also a separate entity. Alan Patten suggests, and we agree, that these two claims need not be exclusive of each other.[117] In our understanding, the Absolute achieves actualization in the free development of human self-consciousness.[118] This interpretation of Hegel has the advantage of not having to overanalyze or dismiss Hegel's language as merely representational when he speaks of God, the Absolute, Spirit, etc., particularly when he does not indicate that this is the case. Rather, Hegel's repeated use of such language suggests that it should be considered in its own right.

For instance, following a Kantian interpretation, Lewis argues that Hegel's account of freedom of thought limits the divine to the nature of the human mind insofar as it requires the individual to recognize that the determinations of thought are one's own and not just the property of the thing thought: "The self-determining character of thinking entails that anything that is meaningful as an *object* is constituted by thinking. Theistic conceptions posit a deity independent of our thinking, thus ultimately posit a God that is subordinate to thinking itself, which entails that it is not properly seen as absolute."[119] This position, however, ignores the possibility that Hegel is sincere or being philosophically explicit when he describes the nature of God as thought or self-consciousness. Similar to Aristotle, Hegel posits a God that is thought thinking thought. In some contrast to Aristotle, in thinking himself, Hegel's God creates the natural and human world. This position does not logically necessitate a God that is neither absolute nor ultimately transcendent.

The case for a transcendent God can be seen most clearly in the first moment of Hegel's discussion of the idea or concept of God in the *Lectures on the Philosophy of Religion*. In this first moment, the divine exists in and of itself. Hegel says, "The first form [is determined] as the element of *thought*, that God is in pure thought as he is in and for himself; he is manifest but not yet issued forth into appearance—God in his eternal essence, present to himself, yet manifest."[120] In the same discussion, Hegel also describes this first moment as being outside of the world and outside of time. In the second moment, God is manifest in the finite world, and in the third the first two moments are sublated. Those accounts of God as a purely human development do not fully take up Hegel's argument of the divine as existing in its first form as universal thought in and of itself. In arguing that Hegel maintains the understanding of a transcendent God, we seek to maintain what has been called a "middle ground" of Hegelian interpretation by Fackenheim and others, wherein the nature of Spirit exists in itself, but this includes its relationship to the natural order and to human consciousness more specifically.

It is relatively easy to see why one would focus on the element of subjectivity within Hegel's philosophy. The nature of the absolute, as Hegel understands it, reconciles both objectivity and subjectivity. Hegel resuscitates the ontological proof for God's existence, saying the concept "is immediately this universal that determines and particularizes itself—it is this activity of dividing, of particularizing and determining itself, of positing a finitude, negating this its own finitude and being identical with itself through the negation of this finitude." And, "Thoughtlessness concerning being prevails to the point that it is asserted that being is not within the concept. It is indeed different from the concept, but only as a determination of the concept . . . this determination is immediately within the concept."[121] Spirit is the universal truth, but the very nature of truth is to determine itself as particularized, as *being*. Correspondingly, as the nature of the absolute results in its manifestation in the created order, particularity and subjectivity are necessary elements in its historical unfolding. It is for this reason, Hegel notes, that proofs of the existence of God can also be teleological, proceeding from the nature of the finite world to the infinite nature of the divine. These two realms are not ultimately opposed, but rather each passes over and into the other. More simply put, each realm participates in the nature of the other.[122] This is, of course, in direct contradiction to Kant's celebrated rejection of these kinds of proofs in his *Critique of Pure Reason.*

According to Hegel, Christians represent their God as particularized even within his own being—three persons in one nature.[123] Correspondingly, the divine manifests itself in the created, particular, and finite realm. To make itself its own object, Spirit reveals only itself, and nothing in the created world—including subjectivity—is alien to it.[124] Hegel explains that the actualization of Spirit requires that it be made manifest in the form most opposed to its nature as universal and infinite. Only in this way will the sublation of difference be fully present within and to it.[125] As a result, Hegel argues that Spirit must be made manifest in a form such that immediate intuition, not speculative philosophy, can achieve certainty of its particular existence. In other words, Spirit must appear in the form of a single human being, as Christ.[126] Moreover, Spirit explicitly reveals itself in human nature: "These extremes, divine and human nature, are not in themselves extremes, but the truth is their identity instead."[127] In Christ, Hegel argues, Spirit shows its nature as incorporating and reconciling all possibilities of difference, including the particular and the finite.

For Hegel, the great strength of the modern world is its recognition of subjectivity, both divine and human. He says, "The great advance of our age is that subjectivity has been recognized as an absolute moment; thus subjectivity is an essential category."[128] Yet Hegel foreshadows, and also responds to, Strauss's concern about the prevalence of modern subjectivity. Hegel tells us that the person who dismisses objective principles of good, replacing them instead with his own preferences, is the root of evil.[129] However, he also notes that a similar effect is achieved when one seeks to accomplish what is universally right or good, without any reference to particular circumstances or interests.[130] Sophocles' Creon is the immediate ancient example, but we need only consider the effects of blindly applying a law without considering the particular details of the crime to see how easily astray such a process may go. Just as what is determined as subjectively good is in no way, or only accidentally, good without taking into consideration the good itself. The good without any reference to the particularity of being is actually devoid of content.

For this reason, while affirming the modern world's recognition of subjectivity, Hegel continues, saying, "But everything depends on how we define it."[131] According to Hegel, particularity and subjectivity are elements of the nature of Spirit and exist in relationship with the absolute and objective. Yet, Spirit cannot be left as finite, but must be brought back into relationship with the infinite. Hegel explains the representational images of the trinity as speaking to the nature of Spirit as being both in and for itself. God as Father speaks to the nature of God as the universal which then determines itself as particular, or as the son of God, but the nature of Spirit is such that both of these moments exist in union. In representational language the return of the son to the father is the work of the Holy Spirit. In more conceptual language, Absolute Spirit is the active sublation of the infinite with the finite.[132] Or as Jaeschke explains, "Hegel's aim is . . . to show that in the idea . . . of the identity of concept and reality as the mode of thinking that thinks itself, the trinity is comprehended."[133] From this, we see the universal as determining itself and determining itself as being. The actualization of Spirit is the reconciliation of these moments as a whole.

The actualization of God in the person of Christ has further intellectual and ethical consequences for human life that are not only subjective in nature. The actualization of Spirit, as reflected in the movement from the infinite to the finite and the continuous reconciliation of both, requires the conscious reflection of the fullness of this truth in human life more generally. In this light, the existence of Christ is the singular example of the entwined identity of God and man that makes possible the knowledge by other humans that this identity is true of their natures as well.[134] Hegel argues that knowledge of Christ through the testament of the community that emerges from faith in his existence is the means by which human beings might come to realize the philosophic significance of being made in the image of God. Understanding the possibility of a reconciliation of particularity with universality leads to a new ethical attitude. As James Yerkes writes, "[it] provides the grounds for human hope and courage in the fact of life's apparent contradictions. It witnesses to a universal divine activity of redemption which teleologically "overreaches" all such existentially endured contradictions."[135] Knowing that the nature of self-consciousness is such that it overcomes the seeming divide between one's finite existence and the infinite scope of one's mind, leads one to the path of discerning how such a reconciliation might be made apparent in an individual's existence within one's communities. In other words, Hegel's account suggests that Christianity presents philosophical and ethical possibilities and obligations to its adherents. Insofar as Hegel is correct that these Christian principles undergird the modern state, these obligations then become the focus of law and ethics and extend beyond the community of Christians.

In the objectively driven Greek ethical world, death and subsequent burial rites provided the appearance of overcoming nature by taking the decomposing body literally out of the mouths of dogs and birds and overlaying it with signs of civilization and rationality. In so doing, the Greek ethical world attempted to negate the finitude present in death.[136] Hegel notes, however, that this attempt by the Greeks to overcome the finite and achieve unity with the absolute, at the cost of particularity, was doomed to fail. Ancient Greeks understood themselves as participating in the nature of the divine as well as that of the beasts, but they believed that these two natures could not be reconciled. In seeking the universal, the Greeks only envisioned part of its nature and were like travelers with a fragmented map. It is with surprising beauty that Hegel describes the end of Greek ethical life:

> Trust in the eternal laws of the gods has vanished, and the Oracles, which pronounced on particular questions, are dumb. The statues are now only stones from which the living soul has flown, just as the hymns are words from which belief has gone. The tables of the gods provide no spiritual food and drink, and in his games and festivals, man no longer recovers the joyful consciousness of his unity with the divine.[137]

It is not the incapacity to achieve unity with the universal in spite of its particularity that accounts for the failure or loss of the Greek ethical life, but rather, the refusal of possible redemption accompanying the particular implies that the Spirit itself is rejected.

In the representational language of Christ's death humans are to understand, according to Hegel, the complete reconciliation of the universal with the finite. Hegel writes, "Death is love itself; in it absolute love is envisaged. The identity of the divine and the human means that God is at home with himself in humanity, in the finite, and in [its] death this finitude is itself a determination of God. Through death God has reconciled the world and reconciles himself eternally with himself."[138] Spirit, the absolute and the eternal, takes upon itself the determination of being fully finite, and, in this, makes possible the reconciliation of our particularity with what is universal.

This is not to say that the finite supersedes the infinite, but rather, in self-consciousness, these two are recognized in unity. The person who sees the possibility of his own universality, through the death of God, then also sees how these two elements are divinely united.[139] This particular soul perceives and seeks the universal for itself.

Spirit as Freedom

Placing emphasis on subjectivity, Hegel's philosophic explication of Christianity brings freedom to the forefront of ethical life. Corresponding to the nature of the absolute as the reconciliation between the objective and subjective, Spirit is also understood as freedom. Strauss remarks that just as the modern world exchanges objectivity for subjectivity, so too does it exchange virtue for freedom.[140] However, for Hegel, as subjectivity is understood in relationship to what is objectively true rather than in opposition to it, so too is virtue taken up and made complete in Hegel's understanding of Spirit as perfectly free.

In the limited terms of practical activity, most people understand freedom as being able to do or achieve what one wants. However, as Hegel, and before him Plato and Aristotle, understood, doing what one wants means to fully understand one's ultimate desires as well as the means of fulfilling them. Even more simply, what we think we want may, when achieved, turn out to be exactly what we did *not* want. The difficulty with human freedom is the possible lack of connection between what one might momentarily and particularly desire, and what one actually and objectively seeks. Therefore, freedom extends beyond our mere practical activity in the world. That we can think untrue thoughts and be captive to our desires means that we might be internally enslaved as well. Hegel points out that knowledge consists of two moments: "first, the fact *that I know*; secondly, *what I know*."[141] Real knowledge, unconstrained by ignorance, requires that what we know corresponds to what actually is and that we know it as such. Our subjective understanding has to correspond with what is objectively true.[142]

Few imprisoned people would consider themselves free, regardless of how true or free their thoughts. As indicated earlier, Hegel believes that one can only be certain that what he thinks is true, is in fact true, if it is made an object external to himself for his consideration. The nature of Spirit is, as Hegel describes, to make itself manifest; "it involves an appreciation of its nature, as also an energy enabling it to realize itself, to make itself *actually* that which it is *potentially*."[143] For Hegel, true freedom requires a full reconciliation between objectivity and subjectivity where the subject seeks the known and true object of his fulfillment and this object is possible for him to achieve. This freedom is the nature of Spirit and, as such, is the end that all human activity ultimately moves toward. Christianity, according to Hegel, is *the* religion of freedom. As Pippin says of Hegel's political ideal, "Essentially, this is also the Christian promise: that there need not be masters and slaves, that, exactly like Christ, each is both master and slave, ruler and ruled, father and son at once."[144] For this reason the Christian ethical account is practical in intention, not merely internal and theoretical. We will take up Hegel's discussion of freedom more fully in the following chapter.

Christianity brings to the forefront, literally, the importance of human subjectivity. While the Jews envisioned a God, the very sight of whom would result in death, and the Greeks envisioned gods who held mortals in contempt, Christianity reveals a god who declares himself as equal, even a friend and, further, fully appropriates human individuality.[145] This subjectivity is inherently connected to freedom. Similar to ancient philosophers, Hegel recognizes that real freedom means consciously acting in accordance with one's true end, an end that may not correspond to his immediate or uneducated desires. By recognizing and highlighting the subjective nature of Spirit, he also understands that individual particularity must be accounted for. All human beings may indeed share the same objective end. But insofar as we partake of the nature of the absolute, we are also individual subjects and this too must be incorporated. Jaeschke explains, "It is not freedom in general that entered the world through Christianity, for then there would be no pre-Christian history insofar as history, according to Hegel, is precisely the progress of the consciousness of freedom. But it is a part of Christianity . . . that freedom be attributed to humans as such, not merely in some limited respect, but as persons."[146] Hegel argues for not just the formal freedom of Plato or Aristotle but actual freedom wherein one's distinct and particular desires can be reconciled and incorporated within what is objectively good. Perhaps too simply, human beings may all have one end, but they reach it through many distinct and equal paths.

Although Hegel defines the nature of Christianity as freedom, perhaps more evidently, he sees freedom as the end of social and political life. Hegel famously notes, "the Eastern nations knew only that *one* is free; the Greek and Roman world only that *some* are free; while *we* know that all men absolutely (man as *man*) are free."[147] Perhaps this is where Strauss derives his equation of Hobbes and Hegel. For like Hobbes, Hegel's political world is one wherein the diversity of human interests and desires are released. While Strauss believes that this development leads to what he describes as "lax moral view," Hegel argues that we will recognize what is objectively good and direct our energies toward this in, and through, our acquisition of freedom.[148]

In a sense, as Strauss suggests, there is a secularization of society. Hegel believes that Spirit, as fully revealed in the Christian religion, is our true end. Yet, he also understands that taking this end seriously requires human beings to be free to appropriate it as they choose. As such, Hegel envisions a separation of church from state.[149] While it is the role of civil society to take upon itself the civic education of children, it seems that our religious education is an entirely private affair. Furthermore, there is no need for religion to be explicitly present in the political sphere, as its principles are taken up in the intent and structure of ethical political institutions.

One might argue that Hegel detracts from the church in favor of the state, thereby demonstrating that our political and earthly lives are of greater, if not of singular, importance. Hegel is clear, however, in his belief that religion is the foundation of human activity, saying:

> The content of religion is absolute truth . . . [Its] concern is with God as the unlimited foundation and cause which everything depends, it contains the requirement that everything else should be seen in relation to this and should receive confirmation, justification, and the assurance of certainty from this source. It is within this relationship that state, laws and duties all receive their highest endorsement . . . and become supremely binding.[150]

Nonetheless, while Hegel argues that religion is the foundation of one's philosophic and political life, religious institutions speak to a different aspect of human nature and belong to a separate sphere.[151] The same philosophic content is expressed in the form of political institutions, on the one hand, and in representational form in religion, on the other. As religion has its form in feeling and in the heart, its very nature is to be particular. Philosophy, however, and logical demonstration proceed by the same path, and laws, which ought to proceed from reason, are, for the most part, universally applied. Correspondingly, the institutions of the state, derived from self-conscious thought, are such that they can and should speak universally to the minds and wills of all citizens in a way that religious codes cannot. As such, Hegel argues that one's religious beliefs and affiliations should be privately rather than publically accounted for.

Hegel argues that the nature of Spirit is its freedom. As Spirit unfolds in the natural world, human beings achieve a greater degree of freedom to the extent that they recognize Spirit's nature as their own or to the degree that they become self-conscious. In ethical life this means the development of political institutions that incorporate the free participation of individuals within a society, including their free participation in whatever religious life speaks most adequately to their understanding and faith.

If Hegel is correct and Christianity is the religion of modernity and the religion of freedom, one is left with the perhaps troubling thought that in order to partake of the self-consciousness and freedom afforded by modernity, one has to be Christian. In this light, Strauss, Kojève, and countless other non-Christians cannot be expected to understand modernity in the same way as Hegel.

We do not think that Hegel's position necessitates this reading for two reasons. First, as we have seen, faith and reason are not opposed, according to Hegel, but rather travel parallel tracks to the same end. Faith apprehends the concept in representative forms, the other philosophically. Hegel demonstrates what he believes to be the development of self-consciousness as it occurs in religion, but also in thought (*Logic*), political life (*Elements of the Philosophy of Right*), art (*Aesthetics*), and history (*The Philosophy of History)*. While it is important in light of Strauss's thought to demonstrate how the foundational elements of modernity are also foundational to a religion that has, as its end, a vision of the absolute, it is also possible to trace the same movement through other manifestations of human life and thought. An individual might achieve the same level of self-consciousness by recognizing the nature and development of Spirit in any of these forms of human endeavor and thought without having to be Christian.

Second, while Hegel argues that the institutions of the modern western world are founded on elements essential to Christianity, he also notes that one's religious life should be divided from the political institutions that one participates in. Hence in the *Elements of the Philosophy of Right* he writes, "the state can have no say in the content [of religious belief]."[152] Hegel understands human nature as fundamentally free, and, as such, he argues that individuals should be left to freely discern and decide the most important of things, including their relationship to the divine. In the same section, Hegel argues that a stable state can endorse the existence of any religious community, even those that oppose the active participation of citizens in a state's political and civil life. A state that has as its foundation the principles of the Christian faith, particularly freedom, is only logically consistent if it grants citizens absolute religious freedom.[153]

The philosopher that Strauss envisions is one for whom philosophy, or the desire for wisdom, is never satiated. From a distance, the kind of sacrifice required for this position exudes a kind of courageous nobility. The person who chooses the philosophic life must admit that he will never achieve the end that he seeks. From Hegel's perspective, this position represents a kind of romantic immaturity. Strauss's philosopher, Hegel might suggest, prefers the chase, and would be unhappy with whatever he caught, regardless of its logic or sense. Hegel recognizes the Christian religion in great contrast to the ancient religions of the Greeks or the Jews. Socrates, for example, may have felt free to investigate the nature of the divine, but he also knew his own nature to be such that he would always know that he did not know.[154]

Strauss critiques Hegel's philosophy as lacking any objective principle that might provide human beings with the possibility of ordering their thoughts and lives. It seems, however, that Strauss did not fully consider the nature of the principle that Hegel's philosophy does explicate. Spirit, while accessible to human thought and understanding is nonetheless absolute in its nature, and all humans have self-consciousness as their proper end. Rather than the radical historicism that Strauss links with Hegel, it appears that Hegel's entire project is, at heart, a reconciliation of human subjectivity to the highest and most absolute of principles. In this chapter, we have sought to show the metaphysical ground of Hegel's position as countering Strauss's charge against Hegel for being a radical historicist.

Perhaps troubling to Strauss, Hegel also argues that the achievement of self-consciousness is commensurate with the achievement of freedom, both in thought and activity. For this reason we next turn our attention to the practical implications of Hegel's philosophy.

NOTES

1. Hegel, "The Lectures of 1824," in *Hegel's Lectures on the Philosophy of Religion, Volume 1,* trans. R.F. Brown, P.C. Hodgson, and J.M. Stewart with the assistance of H.S. Harris. 3 vols. (Berkeley: University of California Press, 1987),106.

2. The account presented here of Hegel's Christianity and the role it plays in his philosophy owes much to the thought and writings of James Doull.

3. Hegel, "Religion and State," in *Hegel's Lectures on the Philosophy of Religion, Volume 1,* trans. R.F. Brown, P.C. Hodgson, and J.M. Stewart with the assistance of H.S. Harris. 3 vols. (Berkeley: University of California Press, 1987), 345. See also, for example, Hegel, "The Lecture Manuscript," *Hegel's Lectures on the Philosophy of Religion,*

Volume III, trans. R.F. Brown, P.C. Hodgson, and J.M. Stewart with the assistance of H.S. Harris. 3 vols. (Berkeley: University of California Press, 1987), 74 and 103–5.

4. Hegel, "Hegel's Lecture Manuscript," in *Hegel's Lecture on the Philosophy of Religion, Volume III*, 74.

5. Leo Strauss, "Three Waves of Modernity," in *An Introduction to Political Philosophy*, ed. Hilael Gilden (Detroit: Wayne State University Press, 1989), 95.

6. Kojève, *Introduction to the Reading of Hegel*, 67. See also, Kojève, "Tyranny and Wisdom," in *On Tyranny*, 160. Although Strauss agrees with Kojève's understanding of Hegel's account of Christianity, he disagrees with Kojève on whether this new ethical account is laudatory. Kojève points to the radical equality made possible by Christianity that transcends all previous distinctions among human beings, including gender, race and class. This, for Kojève, becomes the basis of what he will call the "world homogenous state" (182–84).

7. See also, Leo Strauss. Papers [Box 9, Folder 1], Special Collections Research Center, University of Chicago Library.

8. Strauss, "Progress or Return," in *The Rebirth of Classical Political Rationalism* and "Interpretation of Genesis," in *Jewish Philosophy and the Crisis of Modernity*, ed. Kenneth Hart Green (Albany: State University of New York, 1997). Batnitzky thus says, "Although philosophy can clarify its meaning, on Strauss's reading of medieval rationalism, the law is not derived from philosophic activity. Instead, the law is the prephilosophic context of and framework for philosophy." See Batnitzky, "Leo Strauss and the 'Theologico-Political Predicament'" in *The Cambridge Companion to Leo Strauss*, 50.

9. Strauss, "Progress or Return," in *The Rebirth of Classical Political Rationalism*, 290.

10. Strauss, "The Mutual Influence of Theology and Philosophy," in *Faith and Political Philosophy: The Correspondence Between Leo Strauss and Eric Voegelin, 1934–1964*, ed. Peter Emberley and Barry Cooper (Pennsylvania: The Pennsylvania State University Press, 1993), 220.

11. Strauss, "Progress or Return," in *The Rebirth of Classical Political Rationalism*, 265.

12. Ibid., 248–49.

13. Ibid., 250.

14. Ibid., 249–50.

15. Ibid., 250. See also, Aristotle, *The Poetics*, 1449a, and Plato, *The Republic*, 607a.

16. Strauss, "Progress or Return," *in The Rebirth of Classical Political Rationalism*, 250.

17. Nietzsche, *The Genealogy of Morals* (New York: Vintage Books, 1989), 1.7.

18. Ibid.

19. Aristotle, *The Nicomachean Ethics*, 1102b, 25–30.

20. Tanquay, *Leo Strauss: An Intellectual Biography* (New Haven: Yale University Press, 2003), 169.

21. Strauss, "Restatement," in *On Tyranny*, 200–201.

22. Strauss, "Progress or Return," in *The Rebirth of Classical Political Rationalism*, 257. See also, Strauss, "The Origin of the Idea of Natural Rights," in *Natural Right and History*, 85.

23. Strauss, "Progress or Return," in *On Tyranny* 249.

24. Ibid., 258.

25. Ibid., 256.

26. Ibid., 250. See also, Tanquay, *Leo Strauss: An Intellectual Biography*, 121–22.

27. Machiavelli, *The Prince*, trans. Harvey C. Mansfield, Jr. (Chicago: University of Chicago Press, 1985), 22–23.

28. Strauss, "Interpretation of *Genesis*," *L'Homme* 21:1 (janvier–mars 1981): 6.

29. Ibid., 7.

30. Strauss, "Jerusalem and Athens: Some Preliminary Reflections," *Faith and Political Philosophy: The Correspondence Between Leo Strauss and Eric Voegelin, 1934–1964*, 112. On this point see also, Steven Smith, "Leo Strauss: Between Athens and Jerusalem," *The Review of Politics*, 53:1 (Winter, 1991): 75–99.

31. Straus, "Interpretation of *Genesis*," *L'Homme*, 8.

32. Ibid.

33. Ibid., 15.
34. Strauss, "An Epilogue," *An Introduction to Political Philosophy*, 129.
35. Stanley Rosen, "Leo Strauss and the Problem of the Modern," *The Cambridge Companion to Leo Strauss*, 135.
36. Aristotle, *Nicomachean Ethics*, 1140a, 25–29.
37. Ibid., 1177a, 17.
38. Ibid., 177b, 28–1178a, 12.
39. Ibid., 1145a, 10–15.
40. Ibid., 1143b, 25–1144b, 1.
41. Ibid., 1105b, 1–5.
42. Aristotle, *Metaphysics*, 982b, 1–5.
43. Strauss, "Reason and Revelation," *Leo Strauss and the Theologico-Political Problem*, 153–54.
44. Strauss, *City and Man*, 119. Curiously, in his lectures on Hegel, Strauss contrasts Hegel with Plato on the basis that Plato believes in eternal ideas.
45. Strauss, *Persecution and the Art of Writing*, 105, and Strauss, "The Mutual Influence of Theology and Philosophy," 112. See also Robertson, "Leo Strauss's Platonism," *Animus* 6-8; Tanquay, *Leo Strauss: An Intellectual Biography*, 81, 88–89, 175.
46. Strauss, "Preface to Spinoza's *Critique of Modernity*," in *Jewish Philosophy and the Crisis of Modernity*, 146–47.
47. Strauss, "Restatement," 209.
48. Strauss, "Why We Remain Jews: Can the Jewish Faith and History Still Speak to Us," in *Jewish Philosophy and the Crisis of Modernity*, 312.
49. Meier, *Leo Strauss and the Theologico-Political Problem*, 55. In addition, Meier continues by rightly explaining that Strauss's focus is necessarily political because it is in the political sphere that any philosophic account has to justify itself (64). Further, Strauss argues that all philosophy has to be read in light of the political constraints of a time and by these means the esoteric nature of a philosopher's account might be revealed.
50. Rosen, "Leo Strauss and the Problem of the Modern," 126. See also, Schall, "A Latitude for Statesmanship? Strauss on Thomas," in *The Review of Politics*, 134.
51. Strauss, "The Mutual Influence of Theology and Philosophy," 225.
52. Strauss, "Why We Remain Jews: Can the Jewish Faith Still Speak to Us?," 320.
53. Straus, "Marsilius of Padua," *History of Political Philosophy*, 276–77.
54. Strauss, "How to Begin to Study Medieval Philosophy," in *Rebirth if Classical Political Rationalism*, 221.
55. Ibid., 222.
56. Ibid., 223, and Strauss, *Persecution and the Art of Writing*, 21. See also Tanquay, *Leo Strauss: An Intellectual Biography*, 56.
57. Strauss, "Progress or Return," 228 and Strauss, *Persecution and the Art of Writing*, 19–21.
58. For similar accounts of this deficiency in Strauss's thought, see, Merrill, "Leo Strauss's Indictment of Christian Philosophy," in *The Review of Politics*, 77–105, and Schall, "A Latitude for Statesmanship? Strauss on Thomas," 126–45.
59. Batnitzky, "Leo Strauss and the 'Theologico-Political Predicament,'" 54. See also, McDaniel, "The Nature of Inequality: Uncovering the Modern in Leo Strauss's Idealist Ethics," in *Political Theory*, 333, and Shell, "To Spare the Vanquished and Crush the Arrogant: Leo Strauss's Lecture on German Nihilism," in *The Cambridge Companion to Leo Strauss*, 186.
60. Strauss, "Three Waves of Modernity," 93.
61. Ibid., 94.
62. Strauss, "Interpretation of *Genesis*," 8.
63. Strauss, "Natural Right and the Historical Approach," 103.
64. Strauss, Papers [Box 9, Folder 1], Special Collections Research Center, University of Chicago Library.

65. Strauss, Papers [Box 9, Folder 4], Special Collections Research Center, University of Chicago Library.

66. Strauss, Papers [Box 9, Folder 1], Special Collections Research Center, University of Chicago Library.

67. Strauss, "Three Waves of Modernity," 82.

68. Strauss, "Restatement on Xenophon's Hiero," 205. See also, Strauss, *The Political Philosophy of Hobbes*, 109, f2.

69. See Hegel, *Phenomenology of Spirit*, 178-196.

70. Ibid., 795.

71. Ibid., 113–14.

72. Strauss, "Three Waves of Modernity," 95.

73. Leo Strauss, "Seminar in Political Philosophy: Hegel's *The Philosophy of History*" (lecture, The Leo Strauss Centre, leostrausscenter.uchicago.edu, May 1, 1965)

74. In agreement with Lewis, we have turned to the 1827 lectures as the final formulation we have of Hegel's thought on these concepts. However, we recognize with Hodgson that the broader strokes of Hegel's argument in each of the four sets of lectures he gave appear to have remained relatively stable. See Lewis, *Religion, Modernity & Politics in Hegel*, 107; and Hodgson, *Hegel and Christian Theology* (Oxford: Oxford University Press, 2005), 47. For a detailed account of the sources, see Hodgson's introduction to the *Lectures on the Philosophy of Religion*, 8–40.

75. Hodgson reminds us that the question of religion was always prominent in Hegel's thought, and not something he approached only late in life as a kind of afterthought. See Peter Hodgson, "Editorial Introduction," in *Hegel's Lectures on the Philosophy of Religion, Volume I*, 1.

76. Jaeschke, *Reason in Religion: The Foundations of Hegel's Philosophy of Religion*, 209–11.

77. Hegel, "Introduction: The Lectures of 1827," in *Hegel's Lectures on the Philosophy of Religion, Volume I*, 64. See also, Plato, *Republic*, 510a–511e.

78. Hegel, "The Lectures of 1824," in *Hegel's Lectures on the Philosophy of Religion, Volume III*, 106.

79. Hegel, *The Philosophy of History*, 15.

80. Ibid., 17, and Hegel, "The Lectures of 1827," in *Hegel's Lectures on the Philosophy of Religion, Volume I*, 279.

81. For example, see Hegel, *The Phenomenology of Spirit*, 36–37; Hegel, *The Philosophy of History*, 26.

82. Hegel, "Hegel's Lecture Manuscript," in *Hegel's Lectures on the Philosophy of Religion, Volume III*, 29. See also, Hegel, *The Philosophy of History*, 26.

83. Hegel, "The Consummate Religion: The Lectures of 1824," in *Hegel's Lectures on the Philosophy of Religion, Volume III*, 105.

84. Hegel, *The Philosophy of History*, 33–34.

85. Hegel, "Hegel's Lecture Manuscript," in *Lectures on the Philosophy of Religion, Volume III*, 36.

86. For example, see Hegel, *Elements of the Philosophy of Right*, 1. One can see a similar account in the Plato's image in the *Alcibiades*, wherein one can only see one's soul through the eyes of another. Plato, "Alcibiades" in *The Complete Works*, ed. John Cooper (Indianapolis: Hackett Publishing Co., 1997), 133b.

87. Hegel, *The Phenomenology of Spirit*, 186.

88. Hegel, "The Lectures of 1827," in *Hegel's Lecture on the Philosophy of Religion, Volume 1*, 284.

89. Ibid., 286.

90. Sophocles, *Antigone*, 496–503. See also, Hegel, *The Phenomenology of Spirit*, 457, and Hegel, *Elements of the Philosophy of Right*, 166.

91. Ibid., 468.

92. Sophocles, *Antigone*, 1340–46 and 978–86.

93. "The Lectures of 1827," in *Hegel's Lectures on the Philosophy of Religion, Volume 1*, 290–91.

94. Ibid., 291.
95. Ibid., 299.
96. Ibid., 304.
97. Hegel, "The Lectures of 1824," in *Hegel's Lectures on the Philosophy of Religion, Volume I*, 46.
98. Hegel, "The Lectures of 1827," in *Lectures on the Philosophy of Religion, Volume II*, 387.
99. Williamson, *Introduction to Hegel's Philosophy of Religion*, 301.
100. Zuckert, *The Truth about Leo Strauss*, 154.
101. Zuckert, "Strauss's Return to Premodern Thought," in *The Cambridge Companion to Leo Strauss*, 116.
102. Ibid., 96–99.
103. Plato, "Gorgias" in *The Complete Works*, ed. John Cooper (Indianapolis: Hackett Publishing Co, 1997), 467c–468c.
104. Romans 7:19.
105. Augustine, *Confessions*, VIII, 17.
106. Hegel, *The Philosophy of History*, 35–36.
107. For example, see Hegel, "The Lectures of 1827," in *Hegel's Lectures on the Philosophy of Religion, Volume III*, 180–81.
108. Hegel, "The Lectures of 1827," in *Hegel's Lectures on the Philosophy of Religion, Volume III*, 181.
109. Hegel, "The Lectures of 1827," in *Hegel's Lectures on the Philosophy of Religion, Volume I*, 279.
110. Strauss, "Reason and Revelation," 149. See also Zuckert, "Strauss's Return to Premodern Thought," 96.
111. Hegel, "The Lectures of 1827," in *Hegel's Lectures on the Philosophy of Religion, Volume I*, 270.
112. Hegel, "Hegel's Lecture Manuscript," in *Hegel's Lectures on the Philosophy of Religion, Volume III*, 43. See also, Rosen, *G.W.F. Hegel*, 8–9, 11, and Taylor, *Hegel*, 490–91.
113. Hegel, "Hegel's Lecture Manuscripts," in *Hegel's Lectures on the Philosophy of Religion, Volume III*, 38–39, and "The Lectures of 1824," in *Hegel's Lectures on the Philosophy of Religion, Volume III*, 141.
114. Hegel, *The Philosophy of History*, 14.
115. Hegel, "Lectures of 1824," in *Hegel's Lectures on the Philosophy of Religion, Volume III*, 171.
116. For example, the following scholarly accounts, while divergent on other issues, all agree that Hegel's philosophy denies the existence of a transcendent principle: Thomas A. Lewis, *Religion, Modernity, and Politics in Hegel* (Oxford: Oxford University Press, 2011); Robert Pippin, *Hegel's Idealism: The Satisfaction of Self-Consciousness* (Cambridge: Cambridge University Press, 1989); Paul Redding, "The Metaphysical and Theological Commitments of Idealism: Kant, Hegel, and Hegelianism," in *Politics, Religion, and Art*, Douglas Moggach, ed. (Evanston, Illinois: Northwestern University Press, 2011); Robert M. Wallace, *Hegel's Philosophy of Reality, Freedom and God* (Cambridge: Cambridge University Press, 2005).
117. Alan Patten, *Hegel's Idea of Freedom* (Oxford: Oxford University Press, 1999), 23–24.
118. For similar arguments, see Emil L. Fackenheim, *The Religious Dimensions in Hegel's Thought* (Bloomington, Indiana: Indiana University Press, 1967); Walter Jaeschke, *Reason in Religion: The Foundation of Hegel's Philosophy of Religion* (Berkeley: University of California Press, 1990); Martin J. De Nys, *Hegel and Theology* (New York: T&T International, 2009); Charles Taylor, *Hegel* (Cambridge: Cambridge University Press, 1975); Raymond Keith Williamson, *Introduction to Hegel's Philosophy of Religion* (Albany: State University of New York Press, 1984).
119. Lewis, *Religion, Modernity and Politics in Hegel*, 163.

120. Hegel, "The Lectures of 1827" in *Hegel's Lectures on the Philosophy of Religion, Volume III*, 120.
121. Hegel, "The Lectures of 1827" in *Hegel's Lectures on the Philosophy of Religion, Volume III*, 325–26. See also Jaeschke, *Reason in Religion: The Foundations of Hegel's Philosophy of Religion*, 299-303. For a contrary reading of the proofs, see Lewis, *Religion, Modernity & Politics in Hegel*, 166–67.
122. Hegel, "The Lectures of 1824," in *Hegel's Lectures on the Philosophy of Religion, Volume III*, 110.
123. Hegel, "The Lectures of 1824," in *Hegel's Lectures on the Philosophy of Religion, Volume III*, 127.
124. Ibid., 197–98.
125. Ibid., 233.
126. Ibid., 146. For a detailed discussion of the logical difficulties surrounding Hegel's Christology, see Jaeschke, *Reason and Religion: The Foundation of Hegel's Philosophy of Religion*, 311–36.
127. Hegel, "Lectures of 1824," in *Hegel's Lectures on the Philosophy of Religion, Volume III*, 143.
128. Ibid., 101.
129. For example, see Hegel, *Elements of the Philosophy of Right*, sect. 139.
130. Ibid., sect. 104.
131. Hegel, "Lectures of 1824," in *Hegel's Lectures on the Philosophy of Religion, Volume III*, 101.
132. Hegel, "Lectures of 1827," in *Hegel's Lectures on the Philosophy of Religion, Volume III*, 201.
133. Jaeschke, *Reason in Religion: The Foundations of Hegel's Philosophy of Religion*, 306. See also, Hodgson, *Hegel and Christian Theology*, 135.
134. See Williams, *Introduction to Hegel's Philosophy of Religion*, 167–74.
135. James Yerkes, *The Christology of Hegel*, 123.
136. Hegel, *The Phenomenology of Spirit*, sect. 452.
137. Ibid., sect. 753.
138. Hegel, "The Lectures of 1824," in *Hegel's Lectures on the Philosophy of Religion, Volume III*, 150.
139. Hegel, "Hegel's Lecture Manuscript," in *Hegel's Lectures on the Philosophy of Religion, Volume III*, 63–67.
140. Strauss, "What is Political Philosophy?" in *An Introduction to Political Philosophy*, 55-6.
141. Hegel, *The Philosophy of History*, 17.
142. For a similar point, see Augustine, *Confessions*, I,i,i.
143. Ibid., 17.
144. Pippin, "The Modern World of Leo Strauss," 451.
145. *Exodus*, 33:20; Homer, *Iliad*, and *John's Gospel*, 15:15.
146. Jaeschke, "Christianity and Secularity in Hegel's Concept of the State," 134.
147. Hegel, *The Philosophy of History*, 19.
148. See also, Jaeschke, "Christianity and Secularity in Hegel's Concept of the State," 138–41.
149. Hegel, *Elements of the Philosophy of Right*, sect. 270, and Hegel, "Religion and the State," in *Hegel's Lectures on the Philosophy of Religion, Volume I*, 340.
150. Hegel, *Elements of the Philosophy of Right*, sect. 270.
151. Hegel, "Lectures of 1831," in *Hegel's Lectures on the Philosophy of Religion, Volume 1*, 461–62.
152. Hegel, *Elements of the Philosophy of Right*, sect. 270.
153. For a similar account of the place of religious freedom in Hegel's argument, see Jaeschke, "Christianity and Secularity in Hegel's Concept of the State," 145.
154. Ibid., sect. 107.

THREE

Hegelian Freedom

A significant critique of modernity for Strauss as well as for other conservative commentators is the apparent emphasis of freedom over duty and virtue. Modernity, Strauss argues, encourages people to seek freedom from all externally imposed limitations, including those limits that speak to what is just or good. Laws and institutions that might have previously been used to habituate individuals to ethical behavior are now limited to the protection of freedom and the promulgation of the harm principle. Without any further guide, people are generally left to the private fulfillment of their desires, regardless of how low or base these may be. In this chapter, we will argue that this account of human freedom insufficiently attends to the complexity of modern life, and that Hegel offers a better and more complete account of the possibilities of an ethical life that is consistent with human freedom and with the contemporary moral order.

THE VIRTUE OF FREEDOM

Strauss argues that Hegel's philosophy, intentionally or not, logically concludes in the destruction of any objective principle that human beings might look to as a source of guidance for their ethical behavior and ultimate ends. As noted, Strauss argues that the desire for freedom, a desire that he perceives as being "sold" most powerfully by Hegel, comes to animate our social and political life with dangerous, if not disastrous, consequences. Describing the philosophic consequences of freedom, Strauss says, "Existentialism begins . . . with the realization that as the ground of all objective, rational knowledge we find an abyss. All truth, all meaning, is seen . . . to have no support except man's freedom. . . . Man freely originates all meaning."[1] There can be no rational limits to human activity; no reason for a person to do one thing rather than another.

Individually, this means that one can do whatever one wants, including following one's strongest desire. Politically, this means that would-be-rulers need no more justification for their rule than what it takes to garner power, whether that means persuasive speech or coercive force. Either way, reason can no longer claim to be an arbiter of human passion: "Reason can tell us which means are conducive to which ends; it cannot tell us which attainable ends are to be preferred over other attainable ends. Reason cannot even tell us if we ought to choose attainable ends."[2] With the help of science and a little Euthydemus-like optimism even pre-rational limits, such as the laws of nature, can be undone.[3] Human beings, as rational animals, are replaced and there is no logical way to indicate in writing or in thought what they are replaced by because they must be freed even from freedom. And for some, if not all of us, the experience of the modern world is just as Strauss describes it. Moral standards seem to be increasingly lax, and any argument can be defeated by a simple rejoinder about the relativity of opinions.

However, as we have seen and contrary to Strauss's argument, Hegel tells us that Spirit is the absolute and objective truth; as the foundation of human nature, it is the end that directs all human activity. There is, according to Hegel, an objective principle that humans ought to look to as the source of their activity. Nonetheless, in line with Strauss's interpretation, Hegel also argues that the essence of Spirit and of human self-consciousness is freedom. Unlike Strauss, however, Hegel does not see a necessary dichotomy in understanding the nature of Spirit as both absolute and essentially free. In fact, Hegel argues that Spirit must be free in order for it to be absolute; it cannot be constrained or limited by an external other. Instead, the other is the manifestation of Spirit within which it knows itself. In the *Encyclopedia,* Hegel writes, "In the Other . . . mind manifests only itself, its own nature."[4] The finite world is this other, but the actualization of Spirit is the recognition that this finitude is its own determination. As such, rather than being opposed to Spirit it is, instead, the realization of Spirit's nature as freedom. What might seem to be fully opposed to the infinite nature of the absolute is actually the manifestation of the absolute itself.

The fullest actualization of Spirit thus understood is achieved in the movement of human beings to self-consciousness, which is a corresponding freedom. In *The Philosophy of History,* Hegel tells us that the development of human history reveals the actualization of Spirit. In this account, Spirit's freedom is made manifest to itself through the free recognition of the other that Spirit is its own nature. In other words, when human beings recognize themselves as spirit, and make this nature manifest in their political and social orders, what is other than Spirit reveals itself as spirit and the freedom of the absolute is apparent both in and for itself.

In contrast with Strauss who implies that the modern account of freedom necessitates a freedom from all limits, Hegel argues that reason is freedom; we are only free when we act rationally. Freedom is the reconciliation of an individual's subjective nature with what is objectively true, for it is only when what is subjectively understood of oneself corresponds with what is actually true, that a person exists freely in relationship to one's thought and activity. One can freely imagine all sorts of things about oneself: one is kind, one is athletic, and one is clever. However, when the manifest reality of one's actual life is made apparent in activity in the world, one may very soon realize the unlikelihood of being all of these things. The freedom one imagined was not freedom at all; instead, the individual was enslaved by false opinion. True freedom requires a clear and right understanding both of oneself and the world that one operates in so that the mind and the will are not limited by unanticipated constraints.

This, however, requires that we fully understand human nature as essentially rational and free, and direct our activity to the attainment of a life most conducive to this freedom. The content of our activity has to be entirely our own; it can be neither externally nor internally given. For this to be the case the contents of our wills, the choices we make and act on, must be consciously and purposively decided on. Just as we would not count someone free who merely assumed the laws of his community as his own without reflection, so we cannot count someone free who accepts as the foundation of his activity contingently present desires and interests.[5] In order to actually be free, a person must only will an object after rationally considering and understanding this object as being consistent with the ends of Spirit—with freedom.[6] Hegel writes, the "absolute drive of the free spirit is to make freedom into its object—to make it objective both in the sense that it becomes the rational system of spirit itself, and in the sense that this system becomes immediate actuality."[7] In other words, human beings actualize their freedom only when the objective political order in which they participate and will reflects their own essential freedom.

Insofar as the nature of human beings is their freedom, Hegel argues that the most rational state will be one that accepts and incorporates the actual freedom of its citizens; it is "right" that human beings have "rights." If it is correct that human beings are by the nature of their minds and wills free, then their political institutions should reflect and allow for this freedom. Yet, Hegel argues, the political manifestation of freedom will ultimately not result in radical license, as charged by Strauss, but rather, the tempering of desire with the free choice of the best and proper end. The political community that universally recognizes human freedom and rights habituates its citizens to the understanding that their subjective freedom is part of what is universally and objectively true.[8] These people might realize that it is in their interests to promote the well-being of the state that protects their individual and subjective interests, and in so doing they might achieve what Tocqueville describes as a kind of "enlightened self-interest."[9] However, such citizens must then try to understand what constitutes the interests of their state, and in so doing they may perceive the nature of the state as something good in and of itself, not just a means to their particular self-interest. They are thereby dialectically drawn to reconcile what they personally seek with what they know to be universally and objectively good.

Hegel uses the experience of love to demonstrate his point. It is worth noting the degree to which Hegel's account of love differs from that discussed by Strauss in *Hiero*. While Strauss depicts love as inherently selfish, Hegel writes, "Here we are not one-sidedly within ourselves, but willingly limit ourselves with reference to an other, even while knowing ourselves in this limitation as ourselves. In this determinacy, the human being should not feel determined; on the contrary, he attains his self-awareness."[10] When people love others, they seek to make them happy. In doing this they sacrifice what might have been their previous goals and are made happy instead by the others' happiness. While this might initially happen on the level of feeling, eventually, even in romantic relationships, individuals must rationally discern and will their beloveds' happiness to complete their love. Hegel argues that a similar process should occur in a relationship to the state. Just as one desires the actual good of his beloved, so will the ethical citizen desire the ends of his political community as his own, and act accordingly.

Paradoxically, however, human beings are also free to act in opposition to their rational nature as well. Hegel notes, "individuals, to the extent of their freedom, are responsible for the depravation and enfeeblement of morals and religion. This is the seal of the absolute and sublime destiny of man—that he knows what is good and what is evil; that his Destiny *is* his very ability to will either good or evil."[11] Human reason is the basis of freedom, beginning in the freedom of will that it creates, and, ultimately, culminating for Hegel in political and social institutions that actualize this freedom in the practical world in which people live. If human beings are free to choose, however, they can choose whether to act rationally or irrationally; they are free to act in accordance with Spirit's end and, correspondingly, free not to do so. While Hegel argues that, broadly speaking, human development is consistent with the nature of *Geist*, these developments are determined as rational for a particular time and a particular person or group of people who, in making this determination, may not be aware of the fullness of Spirit's nature.

Strauss's misunderstanding about Hegelian freedom seems to be driven by his acceptance of Kojève's interpretation of the prominence of the master-slave dialectic within Hegel's overall thought and, as a corresponding theme, the desire for recognition. As discussed, Strauss's focus on the seemingly Hobbesian description of early human life leads him to accept that the desire for recognition remains rooted in the passion that is at the basis of the master-slave relationship. This, however, is a misreading of Hegel's overall argument.[12]

First, let us note the points of agreement between Kojève and Hegel. It is true, according to Hegel, that human beings "desire recognition," insofar as they desire to achieve self-consciousness and objective freedom. There is both an epistemological and a political requirement for this recognition. As we saw in the last chapter, knowing something as true requires the confirmation of this truth in the objective world around us. Truths individually accepted must be recognized by others so that one might gain an objective awareness of what was previously only subjectively understood. As Wood puts it, "I learn what I am through the interpretation, by myself and by others, of what I have done. As a spiritual being, I do not exist fully and actually except through these contrary and complimentary movements of 'becoming other' and 'mediating' this otherness, that is, through self-expression and self-interpretation."[13]

Further, as has also been discussed, the attainment of freedom requires the practical development of political regimes wherein people are recognized as free and autonomous bearers of rights. Arguing that the satisfaction of human life requires the full integration of human nature, Hegel does not believe that freedom of the mind is sufficient. In addition, one must be able to practically will what one desires and knows to be the good. Hegel writes, "The will is determined by no means only in the sense of content, but also in the sense of form. Its determinacy with regard to form is its end and the accomplishment of its end. At first this end is only *subjective* and internal to me, but it should also become *objective* and throw off the deficiency of mere subjectivity."[14] The political community that recognizes human rationality grants individuals the freedom to objectively achieve what they subjectively desire.

Recognition by others is an essential component of Hegel's thought. Yet, the quality or nature of the recognition desired and received is transformed as human beings progress through history. According to Hegel, knowledge of oneself or self-consciousness begins in immediate consciousness. In this state, the individual knows himself as singular, without any perceptible distinctions in his being.[15] And yet, this understanding is not accurate. We *are*; but, we also may be hungry, and we may also be thinking—just to name a few of the possible determinations that could simultaneously be true at any given moment. Like the divine, the essence of human nature is both universal and particular. In the previous chapter we explained the relationship of Spirit to the finite and created world. Just as Spirit knows itself in relation to the created other, so the individual knows himself in all of the particular modes of his being or aspects in relationship to something else. Self-knowledge requires recognizing oneself in someone else.[16] If an individual can perceive that another person shares his nature, then that person can be an external and objective stand-in or a way for him to study and know himself. However, in doing this, the individual is also put in a position of noting the differences between himself and others. He learns what he is and that necessarily requires him to determine what he is *not*. The development of self-consciousness occurs for humanity progressively through history. Through the course of history, people become increasingly self-aware, incorporating the truths they had previously understood with greater awareness of their complete natures.[17]

In the master-slave dialectic, human consciousness is just beginning the long process of self-knowledge. An individual may see himself in others, but he has not yet rationally developed any ethical or meaningful distinctions for separating himself from the other. As such, prior to the famous fight for life, or perhaps more properly stated as the fight for death, his consciousness of his similarity to others is the same as losing himself in the other.[18] The individual does not yet have a means to recognize the determinations of his own nature. The struggle for life, however, gives him the grounds for this distinction. The master is different from the slave, and from all animal existence, in that he is willing to die.[19] At this stage of the development of thought, the only meaningful distinction one can understand is the most immediate—life or death. Each combatant seeks to be known by the other as different, as the one willing to die. In being so recognized, the individual is able to know something of himself and gain a level of self-consciousness.

As human beings progress they are able to draw more and more rational comparisons. As they develop greater awareness of themselves through their social and political organizations, they find more nuanced means of distinguishing themselves from others. In the Greek ethical state, sisters and brothers are able to see themselves in each other because of their common ancestry, but, at the same time, have the distinction of their gender as a point of distinction. This becomes the grounds for both their self-knowledge and ethical responsibility, with women seeing their role as being within the family and men taking responsibility for the political community.[20]

In Hegel's later work, *Elements of the Philosophy of Right*, his account of human self-consciousness has transcended the relationships of the *Phenomenology*, indicative of either a development in his own thought or merely a progression from the early communities described in the *Phenomenology* to the ethical state described in *The Philosophy of Right*. By this time the relationship of brothers to sisters is no longer the most important, as humans have moved beyond thinking about the basis of their similarities primarily in terms of shared blood lines. Instead, the relationship of husband and wife takes precedence. Their rationally mediated love for one another takes center stage and is the common bond for spouses to recognize themselves.[21] Hegel, however, still makes gender the important distinguishing characteristic and individuals at this stage understand themselves as male or female and thereby develop their objective roles in the community according to this distinction.

But the family is not the highest moment of this stage of ethical life. The family is the realm whereby immediate particularity and desire find a home. In the state, alternatively, desire is more fully mediated by reason and human rationality is most prominent in this realm. In this sphere, human beings are able to recognize one another as citizens who deserve the same rights and freedom. Recognizing himself in other citizens, the ethical individual perceives the universal element of his nature; he is a rational and free being, deserving of being treated as such. Yet, this individual is able to recognize his own distinctness in the rational differences experienced as a member of a vibrant and diverse political community.[22] The particularity of a citizen's nature is thereby made manifest, understood, and incorporated.

Strauss and Kojève are correct to see the desire for recognition as important to Hegel's argument. However, the focus Strauss places on desire and his interpretation of the role it plays in the Hegelian state is misleading. The desire for recognition is, for Hegel, analogous to the desire for wisdom or philosophy. In seeking to be known by others, people actually seek knowledge of their true natures and, finally, the nature of the highest of things—Spirit. The desire for recognition is the means whereby human beings are spurred, perhaps unconsciously in the beginning, to discover and understand the most perfect object of their thought, *Geist*.[23] Although Kojève recognizes a dialectical relationship between recognition and wisdom, in the end, he places greater emphasis on recognition, saying that the self-conscious individual seeks recognition and wisdom is the means to this end. Hegel understands the correspondence between being recognized by others and the development of self-consciousness as being more fully integrated and entwined; both are means and ends simultaneously.

The desire for recognition manifests itself in the most rational state, not in the form of unmediated passion. Ethical actors do not look for others to perceive the value and worth of their most base and immediate desires. Instead, in being known by the state as autonomous and rational beings, ethical citizens recognize themselves as such and their desires and interests are thereby mediated. Hegel says, "The self-will of the individual . . . in its attempt to exist for itself and in opposition to ethical substantiality, have disappeared . . . it recognizes that its own dignity and the whole continued existence of its particular ends are based upon and actualized within this universal."[24] In seeing that the political community respects the particular choices of individuals, these citizens are more likely to see that it is in their interests to ultimately will the good for the state. Even further, in so doing, their interests are enlarged and reformed. This becomes evident when one traces the desire for recognition through the various relationships Hegel details throughout both the *Phenomenology of*

Spirit and *The Philosophy of Right*. As human understanding develops, a person's understanding of his nature becomes increasingly more nuanced. At first people define themselves in terms of their most prominent passion, the desire to live, but in the creation of the ethical state, they know themselves as rational and responsible members of a political community and are recognized as such.

According to Strauss, the state that Hegel describes is at best illusory or, at worst, debilitating. For, as Strauss explains, a community that recognizes everyone regardless of his or her achievements will no longer be able to motivate its citizens to achieve the requisite wisdom or virtue. The first step in untangling Hegel's response is to see the dialectical relationship that exists between human understanding and the political structures that support it. Political institutions are the products of rational thought. However, as we have already discussed, they are also the means to greater understanding. As the objective representations of what humans subjectively understand, regimes both confirm and develop the understanding and self-consciousness of their citizens. Hegel writes, "Society and the state are the very conditions in which Freedom is realized."[25] Practically speaking, Hegel argues that the work of building new political orders has its impetus in the understanding and will of world-historical individuals. Recognizing the deficiency in existing states, these individuals devote themselves to transforming their political orders into closer approximations of the regime most likely to result in what they understand to be a better, if not the best, human life. Hegel writes, "World-historical-men—the Heroes of an epoch—must . . . be recognized as its clear-sighted ones; *their* deeds, *their* words are the best of the time."[26] As we will see, Hegel does not require that such individuals recognize the full movement of Spirit through human history; it is sufficient that the end they seek is a rational response to the deficiencies in their current political and social orders.

By creating better political regimes, world-historical individuals actualize the nature of Spirit in the world. At the same time, however, the objectification of what is individually understood as better has the effect of further confirming this knowledge, both to these individuals and, perhaps more importantly, to other citizens of these states. Hegel says, "It must further be understood that all the worth which the human being possesses—all spiritual reality, he *possesses* only through the State. . . . For Truth is the Unity of the universal and subjective Will; and the Universal is to be found in the State. . . . The State is the Divine Idea as it exists on earth.[27] In this, Hegel's thought is not very different from that of Aristotle who understood the capacity of laws to habituate citizens to moral activity, whereby doing good things leads individuals to understand, and desire, their goodness.[28] Just as a person perceives and understands himself through the lens of another person, the political institutions of his community also serve to reflect this truth, perhaps even more ably. As the most prominent example of a universal and objective entity, in reflecting on the nature of the state, citizens can be brought to know the nature of Spirit itself.

Yet, the logic of Hegel's argument does not require all citizens of an ethical state to achieve the same level of knowledge, let alone absolute wisdom. As noted earlier, Hegel remarks, "In affirming . . . that the Universal Reason *does* realize itself, we have indeed nothing to do with the individual empirically regarded. That admits of degrees of better and worse, since here chance and specialty have received authority from the Idea to exercise their monstrous power."[29] Hegel's exposition of the ethical state in *The Philosophy of Right* considers the reality of crime and the legal institutions required to ensure justice for those citizens who do not act in accordance with the state's ethical aims. Hegel fully recognizes that the state he describes will not ensure the ethical nature of all of its citizens. The contingencies of the finite world and the real freedom of individuals means that there will always be a need for further education and institutional change to respond to the infinite variety of circumstances that will occur.

The institutional act of recognizing individuals as autonomous bearers of rights is a method of education. By perceiving that this is the true nature of its citizens, whether fully realized or not, the state endorses who they ought to be and thus provides a way by which they might achieve this.[30] Unlike Strauss, Hegel does not believe that the educational value of honor or recognition lies in withholding it until the desired behavior occurs; instead, by recognizing all of its citizens, the ethical state provides them with an objective view of themselves, so that they might seek to individually attain this end. This is not a lowering of ethical standards in order to accomplish a democratic regime, but an invitation to all to participate in an objective good that is only possible within a democratic society.

THE RATIONALITY OF DESIRE

Strauss contrasts human freedom with the requirements of human virtue, suggesting that Hegel's account of freedom is about the license to do what one wants without limit. While ultimately we disagree with this position, one can find ammunition to support this interpretation in Hegel's political thought. For instance, in *The Philosophy of History,* Hegel tells us that the transition from one historical period to another is caused by passionate revolutions. Of these, Hegel explains, "When we look at this display of passions, and the consequences of their violence; the Unreason which is associated . . . with them; when we see the evil, the vice, the ruin that has befallen the most flourishing kingdoms which the mind of man has ever created; we can scarce avoid being filled with sorrow at this universal taint of corruption." History might thus be described as a "slaughter bench."

Further, as we shall see, the nature of Spirit, and the fulfillment of human nature, requires the integration of individual subjectivity into the objective institutions of our political communities. Self-consciousness, Hegel argues, reconciles the subjective and objective elements of Spirit. When Spirit knows itself, it knows the one objective truth. This truth is its whole. However, when spirit is actualized in human beings, they know the one objective truth as it manifests alongside, and within, their particular consciousness. Hegel argues that the realization of spirit in human consciousness requires incorporating these particular and subjective elements in a real and substantial way. Hence, the state that Hegel describes in *The Philosophy of Right* recognizes and allows human beings to freely choose and organize most aspects of their lives. For example, even though Hegel does not go so far as to establish equality of men and women, he nonetheless argues that women should be allowed to choose their own husbands, and that, for the most part, people should choose their employments based on personal talents and interests. Strauss correctly notes the emphasis on particularity in Hegel's account. Yet, the incorporation of human subjectivity is not the unleashing of individual desire that Strauss seems to imply.

This becomes clear in Hegel's description of passion as the most effective motivator of human action and a means to history's development. For, as Hegel points out, if the goal of political thought is to transform political life so that it more fully approximates and encourages human happiness then it is not enough to merely know what is best. One must also have the means and the will to act in accordance with what is true. However, to will something is to desire its accomplishment and as Hegel says, "If men are to interest themselves for anything; they must (so to speak) have part of their existence involved in it; find their individuality gratified by its achievement."[31]

Very few, if any, people can accomplish the ideal of doing what they ought to solely because it is their duty and without achieving any personal satisfaction. Instead, Hegel would say that a person who does what is right because it is his duty, does so only because that particular desire, to act on the grounds of duty, is the strongest. To think otherwise is to delude oneself about the nature of the soul and the grounds of human activity.[32] Having divided the soul into three parts, and having relegated desire to the lowest tier, Plato recognizes that the other parts of the soul are only actualized when desire accompanies the end that they seek.[33] The philosopher is only a philosopher because he desires wisdom. Everything that is accomplished in the human world is accomplished because it is willed and it is willed because it is desired.

That one is passionate about something does not mean that the thing desired is any less good or truthful. When describing the impetus to history's progress, Hegel says, "Two elements . . . enter into the object of our investigation; the first is the Idea, the second the complex of human passions; the one the warp, the other the woof of the vast arras-web of Universal History."[34] As Hegel describes the progression from one historical era to another, he indicates that transformations take place not because of some idiosyncratic preference of a person or a people, but because these people have realized a real deficiency in their current society. While it may certainly be the case that passion can cloud one's judgment, it is also true that one's desires can be invoked in the service of truth.

People construct the institutions of their societies with the understanding or belief that these structures are the right ones. Those who found political regimes presumably believe that these institutions will facilitate the best possible life, if only for their own advantage. When change is sought in society, either small or revolutionary, it is because some element of the population perceives that their social order is not fully satisfactory; the current regime does not assist in the achievement of the best possible life.[35] The person who seeks change is not necessarily wrong or misguided; alternatively, the desire for change may be a recognition that what was thought to be a rational means to the satisfaction of human needs and ends is in fact irrational and not conducive to the goals that have been set out for it. According to Hegel, the world-historical individual is the person who willingly sacrifices everything else for the sake of bringing about a better, more rational, existence for human life:

> Such individuals have no consciousness of the general Idea they were unfolding, while prosecuting those aims of theirs; on the contrary, they were practical, political men. But at the same time they were thinking men, who had an insight into the requirements of the time—*what was ripe for development*. . . . It was theirs to know this nascent principle; the necessary, directly sequent step in progress, which their world was to take; to make this their aim, and to expend their energy in promoting it. World-historical men—the Heroes of an epoch—must, therefore, be recognized as its clear-sighted ones; *their* deeds, *their* words are the best of that time.[36]

The world-historical person that Hegel describes in *The Philosophy of History* is motivated by the desire to transform the political world where he lives into a place that encourages and reflects human happiness to a greater degree.

Interestingly, one of Strauss's criticisms of Kojève's global community aligns with Hegel's critique of this same position, although the way they reach this conclusion is strikingly different. Strauss believes that a political philosopher must seek to understand what regime will be best in and of itself regardless of the practical circumstances of any single place. However, Strauss also notes that when actually effecting laws, the particular contingencies of a regime must be taken into account, and compromises from the ideal will be required: "a given community may be so rude or so depraved that only a very inferior type of order can keep it going."[37] The tone of Strauss's reasoning is in explicit contrast to Hegel, who argues that most, if not all, political communities have yet to achieve the ethical life envisioned in *The Elements of the Philosophy of Right*; nonetheless, the political institutions that do exist are a reflection of the rationality of that people, not their depravity.[38] The particularity so present in the finite world is just as much a part of the actuality of self-consciousness as is the objectivity of thought.

Despite Strauss's argument, Hegel's position, in many ways, is more akin to ancient and medieval thought than to other modern philosophers. Unlike Hobbes, Hegel does not think human reason is a tool used by passion. And, unlike Kant, Hegel would not agree that duty is most properly accomplished only when no pleasure is derived from the act. Instead, Hegel agrees with Aristotle, who says that the goal of education is to create the desire for what is correct and rational. Aristotle's virtuous person desires, and takes pleasure in, ethical activity.[39] So too Virgil crowns Dante at the top of Mount Purgatory, telling him, "Make pleasure now thy guide," as his desires have been ordered to the good.[40] Human beings who are free are not, as suggested by Strauss, driven or enslaved by their passions, but rather, they can be freely moved by desire that is known as rational. Inasmuch as human happiness lies in fulfillment of human nature, the desire for freedom is the most rational of desires, concurrent with the desire for truth. As Garza puts it, "True freedom for Hegel . . . can only exist when the concept of the universal, a truth that transcends the egoistic world of the individual and is embodied in ethical life, is also embodied in the individual subject's conscious purpose."[41] The practical reality of this claim is one that will be taken up in the final two chapters.

While it is true that Hegel believes that the actualization of human nature corresponds with a full reconciliation of thought and desire, such that the individual would desire what is objectively true, Hegel also suggests that in earlier stages of human development there is a similar, if yet incomplete, correspondence between reason and desire. Speaking of world-historical people, Hegel indicates that they need not understand how their activities conform to the goals of Spirit. Such individuals have not yet attained self-consciousness. Nevertheless, they have developed a degree of understanding sufficient to see that their political social orders are inadequate to their satisfaction. Moreover, they conceive of a different form of political life that will more sufficiently address the needs of the individuals it governs. The vision of world-historical individuals is limited. They do not understand the nature of Spirit, and, as a result, the goals they pursue are incomplete. Yet, they do know something of the true and, insofar as they desire to make this manifest in their political realms, their desires are not irrational, even if they are not yet the expression of the full truth. People achieve the absolute ends of Spirit perhaps unconsciously, but they do so through their own free and rational choices.

As noted earlier, freedom requires an individual to fully determine himself in accordance with what he understands is rational. In so doing, an individual externalizes his nature, creating rational political institutions wherein the freedom of individuals is both manifest and protected. Participating in a rational community has the further effect of mediating what would have been a contingent and particular desire so that it is commensurate with reason and with freedom. The mediation of love through marriage is a good example.

The particular love of another is necessarily grounded in some contingency of desire. While there are objectively good reasons for loving one person rather than another, when presented with two candidates who equally meet all objective requirements, most if not everyone will still prefer one person to another. Hegel does not then argue that this contingency makes the free choice of a partner in marriage unethical. Instead, this choice is endorsed and the contingency of the desire that leads one to choose one person rather than another is then mediated by the institution of marriage and made rational. Political communities that recognize the essential nature of human beings as free then incorporate individual subjectivity and even the particularity of desire into universal institutions. These institutions accept this particularity and mediate it such that what was a purely particular desire for one person rather than another becomes the rational foundation of the family and of the political community more broadly.

In the *Philosophy of Right*, when discussing the idea of morality, Hegel asks whether human beings have a right to seek happiness when, as Patten indicates, willing happiness is not the same thing as willing freedom.[42] Hegel responds saying:

> We may ask at this point whether the human being has a right to set himself ends that are not based on freedom, but solely on the fact that the subject is a living being. The fact that he is a living being is not contingent, however, but in accordance with reason, and to that extent he has a right to make his needs his end. There is nothing degrading about being alive, and we do not have the alternative of existing in a higher spirituality. It is only by raising what is present and given to a self-creating process that the higher sphere of the good is attained.[43]

As we shall see in the next chapter, in the discussion of morality Hegel argues that the inward turn of subjectivity is valid insofar as the individual seeks the freedom that is the essence of his will. At this stage in the development of ethical life, however, this inward turn is incomplete because the objective foundation of what a subject should will has not been actualized objectively. The individual has nothing concrete to direct his activities at other than the particularities of his conscience. In ethical life proper, freedom of the will has been made actual in the manifest laws and institutions of the ethical community. When the individual seeks to will the content of his freedom, the ethical community is able to both direct him to proper object of his will and is the place wherein his own will is incorporated and made actual.[44] In some disagreement with Patten who argues that Hegel's ethical individual must only will what is rational, "*all the way down*,"[45] we argue that Hegel's account of freedom allows for and incorporates the particular desires and interests of an individual life even when there is perhaps no objective reason for the choice of one thing over another (e.g., a spouse) beyond the subject's preference. In this we are in closer agreement with Moyar, who writes, "Eliminating contingency is . . . problematic in considering the major decisions one makes in life, such as whom to marry. . . . Those decisions are a function of contingent desires and circumstances. . . . [A] perspective that abstracts completely from our contingent desires will be a perspective in which we do not recognize ourselves or our most important commitments."[46]

Hegel does not perceive a necessary dichotomy between reason and passion or, in more political terms, between duties and rights. Instead, of the truly ethical person, Hegel says, "*duty* and *right* coincide in this identity of the universal and the particular will, and in the ethical realm, a human being has rights in so far as he has duties, and duties in so far as he has rights."[47] For Hegel, the fulfillment of human nature requires a complete integration of all elements of a human life. In Hegel's final ethical state, humans have rights and are free, but in their freedom they desire what is rational and thus take up what are at the same time their duties or obligations. This is not the "hollow freedom" described by Strauss. Hegel quotes Dante's *Paradiso* in the *Philosophy of Mind* to support his argument that human beings can attain the truth. Significant to this discussion is the relationship between desire and reason that the quotation also takes up:

> I see that nought can fill the mind's vast space,
> Unless the *Truth's* light dwell there as denizen,
> Beyond which nothing true can find a place.
> In that it rests, like wild beast in its den,
> When it *attains* it; and it *can* attain,
> Else frustrated would be all desires of men.[48]

Understanding, Hegel argues, is necessary to the fulfillment of human desire, for at the foundation of all human want is the desire to actualize the fullness of our natures as self-conscious and free individuals.

THE PARTICULARITY OF THE STATE

It is necessary to clarify the nature of the ethical state that Hegel envisions. Strauss puts forward the world homogenous state and apprises us of the dangers inherent in this conception. There is the already answered difficulty that it is improbable that all people in a single community, let alone in the world, will have achieved the wisdom required for membership in such an organization. As a result, Strauss argues the emergence of this state will necessarily be tyrannical. Given that many, if not the majority of people in the world, will not recognize the posited end or method of this regime as beneficial, its coming into being will require the presence of a ruler with sufficient strength to overcome all possible disputes. If a world homogenous state were the goal, Hegel would likely agree. There is no way, in Hegel's understanding, for a single political organization to peacefully incorporate the diverse interests and stages of development of all the world's peoples. And for exactly this reason, Hegel does not make an argument for a world homogenous state. Instead, his argument is almost the opposite.

The development of human consciousness and political institutions is logically the outcome of a single rational process, one that humans share with the divine. This, of course, suggests that there will ultimately be great parallels with respect to the development of different communities. However, it is necessary to remember that, according to Hegel, the nature of Spirit is the complete reconciliation of the particular and the universal, which is how Spirit is able to make its own nature manifest in the finite particularity of human life. This means that the actualization of Spirit in human consciousness and institutions requires the real incorporation of subjectivity. The ethical state recognizes human freedom in a complete way. People are free to determine the course of their lives in accordance with their particular upbringing, talents, desires, etc. The presence of these particular moments in human life results in numerous rational responses, all of which can be directed to what is universally true and good.

Just as the particularity of every individual must be freely reconciled with what is objectively true, so too does each political community find its own path to self-consciousness. Hegel writes, "The State is the Idea of Spirit in the external manifestation of human Will and its Freedom. . . . The Constitutions under which World-Historical peoples have reached their culmination are peculiar to them; and therefore do not present a generally applicable basis."[49] Just as Hegel envisions the ethical state as being comprised of a diverse body of citizens, each in pursuit of his particular will in light of the interests of the whole, so too does Hegel envision a diverse and not always peaceful world order, made up of many different states, each of which may define both the end and the means to this end in significantly different fashions. Commenting on

Hegel's consideration of the English Reform Bill, James Doull writes, "In this was a lesson for Germans as to the outcome of the revolutionary period. . . . A free and enlightened Prussian state . . . would have its special character, as the English and French had given their special character to modern freedom."[50] Even if we imagine that all cultures and communities proceed at the same historical pace, something Hegel would contest, the variety of regimes that would necessarily exist would in no way be compatible with a global state.

Evidence for the diverse and continuous development of both individuals and states can be found in Hegel's discussion of international relations, particularly his account of war, in *Elements of the Philosophy of Right*. Philosophically, Hegel says that war is made necessary because of the finite nature of human life and community. Hegel argues that the truth of both moments of the Absolute, the individual and the universal, should be manifest in their entirety. War makes manifest the finite nature of the individual, as a citizen, and the finite life of states: "It is *necessary* that what is finite—such as life and property—should be *posited* as contingent, because contingency is the concept of the finite."[51] Human beings die and political communities are overturned. Wars make these facts an objective reality such that they cannot help but be understood by citizens.

Whatever we might think of Hegel's justification of the place of war in human life, it is evident that Hegel did not imagine a political community would ever reach the state of perfect empire as argued by Kojève. The persistence of war, for Hegel, is evidence that political communities will continue to fundamentally disagree. The particular circumstances of a community, including its geographical, historical, or cultural components, will result in different but still often ethical situations. Of international relations, Hegel says, "states function as *particular* entities in their mutual relations . . . these relations will encompass the ceaseless turmoil of not just external contingency, but also of passions, interests, ends, talents and virtues, violence, wrongdoing, vices. . . . In this turmoil the ethical whole . . . is exposed to contingency."[52] An empire, such as Kojève describes, is not an outcome that Hegel endorses or imagines possible.

There is good reason for Strauss to believe that Hegel's philosophy requires the full realization of his political and ethical thought. As discussed in the previous chapter, the process through which knowledge is achieved requires not merely our subjective certainty of a truth but, further, a reconciliation of what we subjectively believe with what is objectively true. It is not sufficient for one to believe that the angles of a triangle add up to 180 degrees. This belief must correspond with the objective nature of triangles. When an individual is presented with objective and external "proofs" of his beliefs, his knowledge becomes more than just potentially true, but is actualized. Spirit actualizes its knowledge of itself in the created world. Hegel himself writes, "As the *thought* of the world, it appears only at a time when actuality has gone through its formative process and attained its complete state . . . it is only when actuality has reached maturity that the ideal appears opposite the real and reconstructs this real world, which it has grasped in its substance, in the shape of the intellectual realm."[53] One might go so far as to argue that Hegel's claim of absolute knowledge must be incomplete unless he can point to its actualization in the world around him. Hegel himself points to the Napoleonic Wars as evidence of Spirit's pending culmination in the human world.

This account alone, however, is not a fair picture of Hegel's thought. Hegel argues that the philosopher comes to understand what is rational in the actual world around him. This does not mean that the present world has to be a complete and perfect realization of the philosophic idea or concept. Instead, the philosopher is able to see in the nascent beginnings of change the fuller and eternal nature of the concept itself.[54]

In the *Phenomenology of Spirit*, Hegel tells us that the purpose of philosophy or science is absolute knowledge, and he concludes the text with an account of this state of consciousness, suggesting that this knowledge is accessible, at least to him. Yet, he also says:

> it is not difficult to see that ours is a birth-time and a period of transition to a new era. . . . The frivolity and boredom which unsettle the established order, the vague foreboding of something unknown, these are the heralds of approaching change. The gradual crumbling that left unaltered the face of the whole is cut short by a sunburst which, in one flash, illuminates the features of the new world. But this new world is no more a complete actuality than is a new-born child. . . . Just as little as a building is finished when its foundation has been laid, so little is the achieved Notion of the whole the whole itself.[55]

Hegel claims not that Spirit has been finally realized in the world around him, but rather, that in contrast to the world that was disintegrating, he was able to understand the fundamental principles of the community that was to emerge. Correspondingly, Hegel remarks that Plato's *Republic,* although appearing on the one hand as an empty ideal, proves, alternatively, the greatness of Plato's spirit "by the fact *that* the very principle in which the distinctive character of his Idea turns is the pivot on which the impending world revolution turned."[56] Regardless of whether one accepts this interpretation of the *Republic,* Hegel's point is that Plato understood, in the dying moments of the Athenian regime, the nature of the principle or concept that was only then emerging, but not yet explicitly and objectively present. Even further, the Christian foundation of Hegel's work, the absolute knowledge that he claims to have worked out and that he sees being practically developed in the world around him is made manifest in revelation. As such, Hegel is left only to work out what that revelation means.

The appearance of the emerging spirit is not equivalent to its actualization. In addition, the concept has to gain existence in the external world that will continue to demonstrate particular as well as contingent events. Hegel understood that this process remained unfinished during his lifetime. He moreover tells us that nothing as of yet can be said about the nature of America, for it is the "land of the future," and to speculate about the shape it will assume is merely to "dream."[57] Thus Grier writes, "Kojève's end of history thesis has no obvious grounding in Hegel's text."[58] Even Kojève notes that, "at the time of writing the *Phenomenology* . . . Hegel, too, knew full well that the state was not yet realized indeed in all its perfection. He only stated that the germ of this State was present in the World."[59]

When Hegel tells us, "what is rational is actual and what is actual is rational," he is not saying that the rational is now fully explicit in the external world.[60] Rather, his point is that in this world we can find expressions of what is eternally true or Spirit itself. Correspondingly, and as he directly says, this does not mean that everything that externally exists is rational, but that amid the objects of pure contingency, the philosophic mind can find what is essentially true. In the much-quoted passage referred to above, he tells us, "To recognize reason as the rose in the cross of the present and thereby delight in the present—this rational insight is the *reconciliation* with actuality which philosophy grants to those who have received the inner call *to comprehend*."[61] The job of the philosopher, as Hegel claims to have witnessed, is to see the truth as it is made manifest in the world around.

Describing the way wherein the concept is realized in human life, Hegel tells us that its appearance will be as diverse as the circumstances in which human beings naturally find themselves: "the Idea, becomes actual by entering into external existence, it emerges in an infinite wealth of forms, appearances, and shapes and surrounds its core with a brightly coloured covering."[62] In exact contrast to Strauss's world homogenous state, Hegel's concept emerges with beautiful variety. It is thereby difficult to imagine that the task of philosophy could ever be complete, for the philosopher must continuously seek the eternal in a world of continuous change, "for what matters is to recognize in the semblance of the temporal and transient the substance which is immanent and the eternal which is present."[63] While Hegel posits that the modern world, by taking up the lessons of the past in light of what will presently come, can glimpse the notion of Spirit, the ever-changing nature of the finite world means that the actualization of this concept continues in varied forms, ever offering itself anew to human thought and comprehension.

NOTES

1. Strauss, "An Introduction to Heideggerian Existentialism," 36.
2. Strauss, "Relativism," 18.
3. Plato, *Euthydemus*, 294e.
4. Hegel, *Hegel's Philosophy of Mind*, 383.
5. Ibid., sect. 19–23. See also Patten, *Hegel's Idea of Freedom*, 51.
6. Patten suggests that Hegel gives several answers as to how one might objectively determine the content of one's will, including God, spirit, the concrete universal, and freedom. It is out of contention that Hegel understands all of these things as being essentially the same. See Patten, *Hegel's Idea of Freedom*, 94.
7. Hegel, *Elements of the Philosophy of Right*, sect. 27.
8. Hegel, *Elements of the Philosophy of Right*, sect. 141.
9. Tocqueville, *Democracy in America*, 501–6.
10. Hegel, *Elements of the Philosophy of Right*, sect. 8.
11. Ibid.
12. For an interesting account of the relationship of desire to self-consciousness, see Pippin, *Hegel on Self-Consciousness: Desire and Death in the* Phenomenology of Spirit.
13. Allen W. Wood, *Hegel's Ethical Thought*, 46
14. Hegel, *Elements of the Philosophy of Rights*, sect. 8.
15. Hegel, *Phenomenology of Spirit*, sect. 91.
16. Ibid., sect. 175.
17. For useful discussion of the relationship between recognition and freedom and the subsequent diversity of a Hegelian state, see Anderson, *Hegel's Theory of Recognition: From Oppression to Ethical Modernity*.
18. Hegel, *Phenomenology of Sprit*, sect. 179–80.
19. Ibid., sect. 186-7.
20. Hegel, *Phenomenology of Spirit*, sect. 456–60.
21. Hegel, *Elements of the Philosophy of Right*, sect. 161–63.
22. MacDonald, *Finding Freedom: Hegel's Philosophy and the Emancipation of Women*, and Moyar, *Hegel's Conscience*, 33.
23. Hegel, *Philosophy of History*, 33–34.
24. Hegel, *Elements of the Philosophy of Right*, sect. 152.
25. Hegel, *The Philosophy of History*, 41. See also 74.
26. Ibid., 30.
27. Ibid., 39.
28. Aristotle, *Nicomachean Ethics*, 1094b, 5–10, and 1104b, 1–5.
29. Hegel, *The Philosophy of History*, 35–36.
30. Hegel, *Elements of the Philosophy of Right*, sect. 151–52 and 187.
31. Hegel, *The Philosophy of History*, 22.
32. Ibid., 22.
33. Plato, *The Republic*, 580d.
34. Hegel, *The Philosophy of History*, 23. For an excellent account of the nature of the will in Hegel's political thought, see Smith, "What is 'Right' in Hegel's Philosophy of Right?" in *The American Political Science Review*, 6–8.
35. Hegel, *The Philosophy of History*, 23, 25, 28.
36. Ibid., 30.
37. Strauss, "On Classical Political Philosophy," in *The Rebirth of Classical Political Rationalism*, 69–70.
38. Hegel, *Elements of the Philosophy of Right*, sect. 20–23. We will discuss the explicit meaning of these passages at the end of this chapter.
39. Aristotle, *Nicomachean Ethics*, 1104b, 5–18.
40. Dante, *The Divine Comedy: Purgatory*, 132.
41. Garza, "Hegel's Critique of Liberalism and Natural Law: Reconstructing Ethical Life," in *Law and Philosophy*, 380. See also, Allen, "Hegel Between Non-Domination and Expressive Freedom: Capabilities, Perspectives and Democracy," in *Philosophy and*

Social Criticism, 493–512; Franco, "Hegel and Liberalism," in *The Review of Politics*, 838; Mattarrese, "Hegel on Freedom," in *Philosophy Compass*, 170–78; Smith, "Hegel's Critique of Liberalism," in *The American Political Science Review*.

42. Allan Patten, *Hegel's Idea of Freedom*, 50.
43. Hegel, *Elements of the Philosophy of Right*, sect. 123A.
44. Ibid., sect. 138A.
45. Alan Patten, *Hegel's Idea of Freedom*, 51.
46. Dean Moyar, *Hegel's Conscience*, 59.
47. Hegel, *Elements of the Philosophy of Right*, sect. 155.
48. Dante, *Paradiso*, IV, 124–30 as quoted by Hegel, *The Philosophy of Mind*, 440.
49. Hegel, *The Philosophy of History*, 47; see also, Hegel, *Elements of the Philosophy of Right*, preface 20–21.
50. Doull, "Hegel on the English Reform Bill," *Animus*, 54.
51. Hegel, *Elements of the Philosophy of Right*, sect. 324.
52. Ibid., sect. 340.
53. Ibid.,preface 23.
54. For example, for an interesting account of how modern states may differ from the ethical state envisioned by Hegel in *Elements of the Philosophy of Right*, but still embody the Hegel's concept of ethical self-consciousness, see Diamond, "Hegel's Defence of Constitutional Monarchy and its Relevance within the Post-National State."
55. Hegel, *Phenomenology of Spirit*, sect. 11–12.
56. Hegel, *Elements of the Philosophy of Right*, preface 22.
57. Hegel, *The Philosophy of History*, 86–87.
58. Grier, "The End of History, and The Return of History," 133.
59. Kojève, *Introduction to the Reading of Hegel*, 97. See also Peddle, "Hegel's Political Ideal: Civil Society, History, And *Sittlichkeit*," 130.
60. Hegel, *Elements of the Philosophy of Right*, preface 20.
61. Ibid., preface 22.
62. Ibid., preface 21. See also, Hegel, *The Philosophy of History*, 79.
63. Ibid., preface, 20.

FOUR

Modern Morality

Perhaps the strongest critique one can level against Hegel's political philosophy, one that is implicit in Strauss's argument, is that the ethical state that Hegel speaks of does not exist and it seems unlikely to occur in the near future. Even if Strauss does, as we have discussed, misconstrue elements of Hegel's thought, are we not forced to see the justice of his overall attack? Is it really possible to look at the contemporary world and credibly claim that most humans are not only more ethically aware, and thereby morally better than counterparts in previous ages, but actually wiser as well? As Thomas Pangle, a noted student of Strauss, writes, "Beyond the problem of the dwindling of the spiritual resources required for liberal republican energy and stability—a problem even on the premises of the moderns—there lies the even more profound human problem of cultural shallowness and growing spiritual emptiness." [1] Strauss might argue that the negative elements perceived in modern culture are logically necessitated, if not intended, by Hegel's thought. Having accepted the historical thesis that is at the root of Hegel's argument, the contemporary world has relinquished all reasonable grounds for censoring human behavior; as a result, we are left free to do as we like.

Not seeing the development of the ethical state, or even a more ethical state, Strauss emphasizes what he takes to be the unintended consequences of Hegel's philosophy. In this chapter, we will address Strauss's fears of a modernity bathed in the light of a Hegelian history. We argue that the crisis that Strauss points to is not the result of Hegel's thought, but a moment of history that Hegel predicted. In brief, we argue that the complete articulation of Hegel's ethical state has not been realized. Even so, in the following chapter we will provide evidence that, despite the prevalence of a Hegelian "morality," the modern world shows signs of ethical progress as well.

THE CONTINUATION AND COMPLEXITY OF HISTORY

Strauss, or any sensible individual, might point out that Hegel's image of an ethical state has not come to pass. Instead, political communities, which recognize the inherent freedom of their citizens, likely contend with the fact that despite having been granted the right to govern themselves, many choose not to, forgoing even the right to vote. We argue that this criticism is taken up within Hegel's thought, most specifically, in the stages of development that Hegel describes in *Elements of the Philosophy of Right*. Specifically, we believe that many elements of modern culture more fully manifest the stage Hegel describes as morality rather than the ethical state that Hegel's thought points us towards.[2]

Our argument rests on two points. The first is a reminder that Hegel understood that what he recognized about the possibility of human ethical and political life would not be manifest in the near future. In light of the argument of the previous chapter, we understand that the ethical world that Hegel predicts will not appear in any final form, for the particularity of human life and the contingency of the finite world will necessarily result in a variety of ethical forms of community. The state described in *The Philosophy of Right* and the stages it progresses through are idealized and yet to be worked out in a particular human community. Given that Hegel only perceived the beginning of this movement two hundred years ago, it is perhaps overly optimistic to expect a clearer manifestation of what he understood so quickly. As such, the contemporary era shows elements of all three of the types of right or justice described in *The Philosophy of Right*, but, we argue, Hegel's account of morality is often dominant.

The second, perhaps more difficult, argument that we will make is that the modern world is not as irreconcilable with Hegel's ethical state as Strauss envisions. The seeds of the rational state, which Hegel first identified, have already begun to reveal themselves. Following Hegel's advice, we will seek to elucidate the form of the rational in the present. For the most part, we will take this discussion up in the next chapter. Here we explain how the current social world still approximates the spirit of morality that Hegel says conceptually and often practically precedes a fuller ethical development.

First, we must briefly restate our critique to the "end of history" argument. Hegel's position is not that his capacity to perceive the full nature of Spirit meant that its actualization in this world had come to its complete fruition. Rather, events in Hegel's world pointed to what he took as the eventual resolution of Spirit in the human world. In fact, Hegel points, in his own time period, to the yet unconcluded nature of the sphere of abstract right, a form of justice wherein property rights are dominant, saying:

> it must be nearly one and a half millennia since the *freedom of personality* began to flourish under Christianity and became a universal principle for part—if only a small part—of the human race. But it is only since yesterday, so to speak, that the *freedom of property* has been recognized here and there as a principle—an example from world history of the length of time which the spirit requires in order to progress to its self-consciousness, and a caution against the impatience of opinion.[3]

Even though only a portion of Christians, let alone of all human beings, accepted the element of subjectivity that emerged from the Protestant reformation, and even fewer had recognized the practical necessity of developing this concept into the sphere of rights and property, nevertheless something within Hegel's age was yet able to direct the mind to its final resolution of spirit, through the stages of abstract right, and morality, to ethical life. Later in his life, Hegel subsequently turns his attention to the English Reform Bill as a way to educate the Prussian people on the possibility of liberal reform that sidestepped populist revolution.[4]

This point can be clarified if we examine, in some detail, the nature and fall of one of Hegel's world-historical periods. Given Strauss's suggestion that we turn our attention to the ancient world, it is perhaps appropriate to examine how Hegel suggests this world existed and why it inevitably fell. In so doing, we will see that the clearly delineated line of history that Hegel suggests is further complicated when the history of an actual people, even when understood philosophically, is taken into account.

Hegel describes the ancient Greek ethical state as predominantly focused on objectivity.[5] It is Hegel's further understanding that this is an objectivity rooted in immediacy.[6] The Greek order is the first true manifestation of spirit in human social life, yet it emerges here as in its adolescence, and, just as a child might wholly devote himself to an external end without reflection on the nature of himself or the end he seeks, this emergent self-consciousness in Greece is not yet reflective.[7] Using the poetic example of *Antigone*, Hegel explains that, in this era, women and men are defined by their immediate biological natures and find their "homes" in the objective institutions most closely aligned with themselves: Antigone will preserve her family, while Creon seeks only the ends of the state.[8]

Hegel's point is that, at this stage, individual citizens are content to devote themselves to the universal rules laid out in law and, more importantly, custom. We might think of Cephalus in the *Republic*, who knows and attempts to do what the poets say but is hard-pressed to explain what they mean.[9] Initially, at least, there is no tension between the will of individual and the will of the ethical community that he is a part of, for the individual accepts his role without question. All in essence are like Antigone or even Creon, not knowing or questioning the theoretical content of the laws they endorse.[10] A purely democratic form of government, Hegel argues, is the logical and necessary result of this predisposition:

> the interests of the community may, therefore, continue to be entrusted to the will and resolve of the citizens; and this must be the basis of the Greek constitution; for no principle has as yet manifested itself, which can contravene such Choice conditioned by Custom, and hinder its realizing itself in action. The Democratic Constitution is here the only possible one.[11]

The individual and the state, the particular and the universal, present themselves as an unmediated reconciliation and an immediate type of self-consciousness.[12]

The apparent self-consciousness present in this world, as unthinking, is necessarily unstable; self-consciousness, by its very nature, must be reflective rather than immediate. Unreflective individuals, who are united in their passions and wills for the sake of the community, may form the perfect basis for direct democracy. However, the nature of democracy is such that citizens must eventually come to think about their individual essences in light of the larger whole. Hegel notes, "thought—the subjective Universal—menaces the beautiful religion of Greece, while the passions of individuals and their caprice menace its political constitution. . . . Thought, therefore, appears here as the principle of decay."[13] In short, democracy requires the active political participation of its citizens; they must take up and *create* the will of the whole.

Interestingly, Strauss recognizes the movement from custom to a more philosophic life in ancient Greece. When natural right is understood properly, Strauss says, we understand, like the ancients, that certain things are right or wrong, good or bad, according to a teleological understanding of nature.[14] Moderns have dismissed this account, but Strauss suggests that there were other, earlier people for whom the idea of a universal account of nature was not yet possible. Strauss writes, "Prior to the discovery of nature, the characteristic behavior of any thing or any class was conceived of as its custom or its way. . . . Barking and wagging the tail is the way of dogs, menstruating is the way of women, the crazy things done by madmen are the way of madmen just as not eating pork is the way of Jews."[15] Once philosophers discovered nature, however, it was then possible to think about these "ways" in light of the object's natural ends or purposes.

As both Strauss and Hegel understand, a rational human life requires more than just obedience to ancient laws and traditions. Actions in response to particular circumstances have to be decided on, and in so doing distinct positions emerge from what was, at first, imagined as a homogenous entity. In the *Phenomenology* Hegel points to the poetic example of Antigone's clash with the objective laws of the state to demonstrate the flaw in Greek society. In *The Philosophy of History*, he tells us that the very foundation of ancient Greece's political life contained the seeds of its destruction. The insight of the "seven sages," particularly the great lawmaker Solon, set the precedent for virtue but also wisdom as the basis for the Greek city-state.[16] Once unfurled, the power and freedom of the human mind could not be retracted. Greek assemblies premised their decisions on majority votes that required the individual to have the capacity not merely to see what was right and true, but to understand it sufficiently and be able to persuade others of his or her correctness. The sophists were a direct and necessary result of the greatness of the Greeks as well as the clearest indicator of its eventual decay.[17]

Practically speaking, the movement away from custom allowed greater scope for the influence of charismatic individuals to persuade the masses of their positions, resulting in fewer actions directed to the common good and many more activities directed to the personal good of certain individuals. The will or good of the city became the will and good of the individual who was able to speak most persuasively, regardless of the content of his aims, for "the expert Sophist knew how to turn the subject of discussion this way or that at pleasure, and thus the doors were open to all human passions."[18] And while Greek city-states were never unified in their ends, except for the brief period of the Persian war, the introduction of sophists and the assertion of the particularity of human desire as an appropriate arbiter of the good meant that peaceful co-existence was no longer possible. Hegel argues that the Peloponnesian War was the beginning of the practical and necessary downfall from greatness for Greece.[19] We need only to think about Thucydides' account of the Melian dialogue and Athens' assertion that justice is merely the advantage of the stronger to see the principles that Hegel describes in action.[20]

The sophists and the personal ambition of men like Alcibiades represent the destruction of ancient Greece. Yet, and importantly, this ethical decay was even present in the more philosophically satisfactory form of Socrates. Hegel argues that the subjectivity that dominates the concept of morality is an essential aspect of human nature. A world that denies an individual the power to determine for himself the nature of right and wrong denies human beings their completion. Recognition of political freedom and equality is based, as Aristotle notes, on the capacity to govern oneself and, thus, the capacity to make one's own determinations regarding the nature of the good. The individual who recognizes this power within himself can no longer be the unconscious follower of law or the enthusiastic adolescent who lives what he implicitly accepts as good without consciously reflecting on why this might be. Hegel says, "Socrates is celebrated as a Teacher of Morality, but we should rather call him the *Inventor of Morality*. The Greeks had a *customary* morality; but Socrates undertook to teach them what moral virtues, duties, etc., were. The moral man is not he who merely wills and does what is right . . . but he who has a consciousness of what he is doing."[21] Socrates, according to Hegel, endorses the position of subjectivity over and against the Greek objective order. One need only think of the erotic play that courses through the Platonic dialogues to realize that Hegel's point may not be that far from the truth. Socrates, as much as or even more than the sophists, disrupted the immediate justice of the Greek ethical order and, in this view, it is not surprising that he is put to death.

Ancient Greek ethical life is overcome by the awakening of individual subjectivity in its philosophic and ethical life; it is overcome by the emergence, at least in a nascent form, of morality. Yet, growing out of what is merely the appearance of ethical life, or ethical life as it might most immediately and naturally exist, the next stage is not ethical life proper. Instead, the principles of objectivity must be further developed in human consciousness so that one might achieve a self-conscious awareness of one's true nature. In response to the emergence of individuality, the Roman Empire was constructed as an abstract universal principle under which all subjectivity might intentionally be subsumed.[22]

What becomes clear in the examination of the downfall of Greek ethical life is the degree to which the various "ethical" categories, as defined by Hegel, exist interdependently with one another in the course of actual history. When describing abstract right, Hegel suggests that it first finds its political expression in the Roman world and its focus on the legal rights of the person.[23] Yet, Hegel correspondingly tells us that the preceding era, that of Greek ethical life, falls because of the invention of morality in the subjectivity present in Socrates. When describing morality in *Elements of the Philosophy of Right*, Hegel writes of Socrates, saying, "When the existing world of freedom has become unfaithful to the better will, this will no longer seeks to find itself in the duties recognized in this world and must seek to recover in ideal inwardness alone that harmony which it has lost in actuality," and "Socrates made his appearance at the time when Athenian democracy had fallen into ruin. He evaporated the existing world and retreated into himself in search of the right and the good."[24] While abstract right, morality, and ethical life, are described as following conceptually one from the other, their historical manifestation is not so neat. Human life admits to an array of these elements in every era of its existence. The straight line of history that so many scholars read as Hegel's projection is too simplistic to actually account for human existence.

Hegel presents the unfolding of Spirit in human life in accordance with what would be its logical manifestation. While the same logic plays out in the development of individual consciousness and in the consciousness of particular nations, each person and each regime works at its own pace and from its own beginning point. Correspondingly, each regime is made up of a multitude of individuals each singularly making his own journey. Hegel lived at the time when the full nature of the absolute revealed itself as the complete reconciliation between objectivity and subjectivity. Yet, despite what Hegel believed to be the proper end of political life, at any given moment in any given place, one might discover any of the three stages of ethical life. Although political communities, as a whole, will move in accordance to the general trend that Hegel describes, the contingency of nature and individual subjectivity will necessarily result in a much messier picture. In *The Elements of the Philosophy of Right*, Hegel says that when one examines the concept of right alongside its practical embodiment in the world "what we obtain . . . is a series of thoughts and another series of existent shapes, in which it may happen that the temporal sequence of their actual appearance is to some extent different from the conceptual sequence."[25] We are therefore reminded that Hegel strives to show what is rational in the temporal and finite. It does not follow that the finite world obeys the detailed path that Hegel describes. Alternatively, given the nature of the finite and the contingency present therein, we should expect there to be significant variations.

Although Hegel sees the absolute moment of history conceptually, its accomplishment in human history is even more complicated than Hegel's own writing style. He understands that self-consciousness is the full reconciliation of objectivity and subjectivity, but this is not fully actualized within the contemporary world. Instead, we argue, that morality, as Hegel describes it, is the dominant form of right found in the western world. It is this stage of human development, we believe, that Strauss finds so problematic.

In Strauss's lectures on *The Philosophy of History*, he makes morality his focus, suggesting that Hegel accepts Kant's definition of morality. Hegel's moral individual is, Strauss says, "A man who does his duty because it is his duty and he does not want to be rewarded for doing his duty . . . So the truest moral men do not want a reward for their virtue, they do not want external happiness, they are satisfied with a good conscience."[26] When he turns his attention to ethical life, Strauss spends very little time explicating it, but rather describes it as an "ethos" or objective morality. In other words, he says ethical life proper speaks to the objective institutions of a regime without any reference to the satisfaction of individuals within these institutions.[27] Strauss then proceeds using these definitions of morality and ethics to indicate that Hegel's account of each, particularly in relationship to history, are questionable if not just insufficient. Specifically, Strauss argues that given the "slaughter bench" of history, the moral individual does not get his just desserts. Instead, the moral man is "run over" by history, but as he is moral, he will not be concerned by the injustice done to him, for his good conscience is reward enough. He thereby implies that Hegel's argument insufficiently attends to the actual people who are caught up in the historical process.

This account, however, does justice neither to Hegel's understanding of morality and its limits nor to the fuller account of right that is present in Hegel's ethical life. The injustices done to individuals throughout the historical process are not something that Hegel dismisses; instead, he describes the image of them as a kind of "mental torture."[28] In light of all of the terrible things that have happened historically, Hegel's point is to seek some kind of rationale or explanation—a greater end to which all of this destruction might lead. He does not excuse it or seek to justify it, but given that it is, and given his understanding that Spirit rules the world, he seeks to find Spirit or reason within it. Moreover, in *The Philosophy of History* Hegel explicitly criticizes morality, indicating that he does not accept it as the sole foundation of virtue, writing of moral reflection, "it is not the interest of these sentimentalities, really to rise above these depressing emotions; and to solve the enigmas of Providence. . . . It is essential to their character to find a gloomy satisfaction in the empty and fruitless sublimates of that negative result."[29] Further, the end that Hegel identifies history as moving towards, that of ethical life, is the solution for the very problem Strauss identifies. In ethical life, the individual is not discounted or thrown away, but rather finds himself fulfilled within the political order that he is a part of. In what follows, we will delineate these points more fully.

FROM ABSTRACT RIGHT TO MORALITY

In *Elements of the Philosophy of Right,* Hegel describes the progression of social and political life through three stages: abstract right, morality and, finally, in the highest state of political development, ethical life. In the culmination of human development, individual subjectivity is compatible with, and supportive of, the universal and objective order. The political world endorses human particularity by recognizing and protecting individual rights; and the individual, in his freedom, sees the ends of the political order, and even further, the objective good, as his own. However, there are two prior stages of the concept of right and its attending shapes that Hegel argues precede the development of this state, which we will describe below.

Abstract Right

In the stage of abstract right, the objective moment is most prominent. Its focus is individual rights, in and of themselves, but with an abstract, objective understanding. The individual is recognized as a person and instructed to respect the rights of others. The actual nature of an individual's actions within the sphere of his legal rights, as determinant and subjectively defined, is of no concern in the realm of abstract right: "In formal right . . . it is not a question of particular interests, of my advantage or welfare, and just as little of the particular ground by which my will is determined, i.e., of my insight and intention . . . everything which depends on particularity is here a *matter of indifference.*"[30]

As a philosophic description of the nature of the will, *The Philosophy of Right* focuses on the movement of a person's practical rather than theoretical intellect. The will, by nature, has to do with thought in relationship to practical or external activity. In abstract right, one understands oneself as a yet undetermined bearer of rights. Freedom is understood as wholly universal and without any significant grounds for its particularization. Yet, this understanding must find a means for its practical development in the social and political world. In Hegelian language, it must exist both in and for itself. Hegel says, "the personality of the will stands in opposition to nature as *subjective*. But since personality within itself is infinite and universal, the limitation of being merely subjective is in contradiction with it . . . Personality is that which works to overcome this limitation and to give itself reality—or what amounts to the same thing, to posit that existence as its own."[31] The practical actualization of the will in abstract right occurs in the ownership of property. A person's freedom is invested in objective "things," thereby affecting the will in the most objective fashion as is possible. Further, by imposing their rights or freedom on objective things, people are able to supersede their own internal subjectivity; they literally become objects for themselves.

One might think of early modern political philosophers, like John Locke, as providing a "contemporary" philosophic basis for this stage of political development. As Locke says, "our lives, liberty and estates" are property and, as such, things to which one has rights. Hegel agrees, explaining that at this stage of ethical development, anything can be understood as property as long as it can be thought of as distinct from one's will, including one's life, body, intellectual accomplishments, and even religious observances.[32] According to Hegel, the individual overcomes the particularity of himself and the world around him, making all determinant things potential objects to be taken up and overcome by his infinite and universal will. Locke says, that "reason is appropriation," and, of abstract right, Hegel replies, "Not until he has property does the person exist as reason."[33]

The difficulties of such a position are perhaps self-evident and stem from the universal and abstract nature of right here understood. If human will is believed to be universally and objectively free without any further determinations, and the external and particular world is the space wherein one can exert this freedom, there will necessarily be collisions between what one person wills and what others will. Further, and perhaps most importantly, there will be collisions with what is good in and of itself.[34] While an individual may understand his will as perfectly objective and universal, this position is not accurate, and thus not actually objective. It is yet a particular will that must practically contend with the particularity of other wills asserting the same, mistaken, understandings. The subjective element of human nature must become an object of understanding.

According to Hegel, it is through inevitable acts of wrong, unintentional or criminal, that human beings come to understand that they are not objective forces, but rather particular and contingent beings.[35] Individual subjectivity is thereby highlighted in human consciousness, and these individuals recognize their subjective natures as possible grounds for their ethical activity, transitioning into the sphere of morality. The moral will realizes that it, as a subject, is the basis for its activity. As a result, its subjective inclinations, purposes, and intents become all-important. It is no longer sufficient to merely conform to objective laws. Instead, these laws must pertain to an individual's understanding of what is good. While clearly idealized when stated so briefly, Hegel's point is apparent. When people unthinkingly infringe on the good of another, even if their actions conform to the objective letter of the law, recognizing the harm they have caused results in a movement of conscience. For most thinking and feeling beings, this movement forces them inward so that they might recognize their subjective obligations.[36] The result is ultimately a fuller account of right, for, as Hegel says, "Only in the will as subjective will can freedom, or the will which has being *in itself*, be actual."[37]

Morality

The moral will, seeing that it cannot depend on external and objective laws to determine the nature of justice, turns to the inner court of its purpose, intent, and conscience. As Franco puts it, in morality action "comes to be ever more thoroughly penetrated by the self."[38] In the sphere of abstract right, actions are determined by their objective manifestation, as in the ownership of property and corresponding laws and institutions. In the sphere of morality, the individual seeks to determine that the acts of his will are truly his own, the work of his subjective determinations. In this, the individual will moves to actions that seek to express greater and greater universality, for it is only in willing what one individually recognizes as fully reasonable that a person can be certain that the content of his will is his own subjective end, and not an end that has been merely given to him, either by his community or his own natural being. In moving to such extreme universality, however, without properly incorporating either the rationality of the particular community that he lives in or the rationality of his particular desires, the moral person wills a universal that is empty of content. Insofar as he must will, this content is then determined by the extreme subjectivity of his conscience. In the following we will work through Hegel's account of the stages of morality so that our argument concerning the correspondence of the contemporary era with this concept might be more clearly elucidated.

Abstract right was determined as insufficient because the individual's subjective will was not considered. In morality, every act is understood to correspond with some subjective purpose. When this purpose is investigated, the individual's inward movement is furthered, as he seeks not merely to know that he caused the action, but that it was his intent in so acting. Although Hegel argues that one is responsible for all the consequences of an act that might be rationally projected, when examining intent, he notes that the moral individual seeks his more particular end or motive. In this stage of subjective freedom "the *right* of the *subject* to find its *satisfaction* in the action" is highlighted.[39]

In the first moment of its development, the subjective will takes as its point of departure his natural subjective existence or the fulfillment of his particular desires, broadly understood as a person's welfare or happiness. Having moved to consider the nature of the will as his own, the moral subject has not yet fully developed to the point of recognizing that the essence of his subjective will is its universality; he is yet grounded in the given and particular content of his natural existence.[40] Inasmuch as the subjective will takes its universality into consideration, it is the general welfare of all people that it considers. The movement to self-consciousness, however, is a greater and greater recognition of the nature of the will as free; as such, to be so particularly determined is not the final end of the will even in the stage of morality.

Importantly, Hegel's argument is not that the happiness or welfare of a particular person or people is irrelevant for the purposes of freedom. Instead, as we have seen, he argues that ultimately we must find our particular satisfaction within our freedom and this includes our satisfaction as physical beings. Nonetheless, these contingent and particular needs have not yet been sublated so that they correspond with an ethical world wherein they find their rational satisfaction. Correspondingly, the objective world of external institutions and laws has not yet developed beyond the stage of abstract right. And legally, individuals are still considered in terms of their objective rights, such as the right to property. In other words, the internal and subjective will and the external and objective world have not yet been mediated such that self-consciousness exists both *in and for itself*. As a result, in this stage of morality, the well-intentioned individual who seeks the welfare of all often comes into conflict with the external rights and freedoms of others and Hegel writes, "a *moral intention*—cannot justify an *action which is wrong*."[41]

As a result of this conflict between morality and right, the moral individual seeks to further universalize his will such that the subjective will only wills what it understands to be right. The good thereby becomes the proper object of the moral will's intent. However, the good so understood stands in some opposition to the will; in seeking the welfare of all, the subjective will trespasses right and thereby errs. It then posits the good as its end, but the yet universalized subjective will that has not sublated its particularity or made this manifest in the objective external world. The will, at this stage, is not in conformity with the good. Instead it stands in relationship to it, knowing that the good is what it *ought* to seek.[42] That one understands that one ought to will something suggests that there is some division between what is actually willed versus what should be willed. Further, the good is here posited as the essence of the will's universality, and without any particular determination, it only exists in the thought of the individual. As such, even when one does will what one ought, determining the content of this "ought" is the business of the individual, who may make the correct determination or who may not.[43]

Leaving aside whether Hegel's critique of Kant's categorical imperative is adequate, Hegel argues the abstract law of doing one's duty for duty's sake without any further grounds of determining the nature of this duty, than that it might be willed universally without any contradiction, results in an empty formalism. The good will, which seeks the fulfillment of a law universally understood, must find the grounds for acting somewhere, and ultimately this will finds the necessary content for activity in its own subjective preferences.[44] For example, the good will seeks the welfare of all, and in its practical activity would seek to will only what it might will universally, regardless or even despite its own particular desires. But, as Hegel points out it has not yet been rationally determined or accepted that the welfare of oneself or others is in fact the content of the good. Instead, this is a naturally given content that the subject has adopted as his own. Ultimately, Hegel argues the moral individual falls back on his subjective and particular conscience as the means by which he might determine his good acts. Commenting on the nature of the conscience at this stage, Hegel says:

> *Conscience* expresses the absolute entitlement of subjective self-consciousness to know *in itself* and *from itself* what right and duty are . . . it also consists in the assertion that what it thus knows and wills is *truly* right and duty. . . . But whether conscience of a *specific individual* is in conformity with this Idea of conscience, and whether it *considers* or declares *to be good* is actually good, can be recognized only from the *content* of this supposed good.[45]

The will that sought pure universality is thereby moved to posit its own particular subjectivity as its end.

THE MORAL WORLD AS STRAUSS'S MODERN WORLD

In the description of morality, we catch a glimpse of the modern world as described by Strauss. This is a world that Hegel tells us is philosophically defined by his forbearers, like Rousseau or Kant, but which Strauss describes as proceeding from Hegel's thought through his philosophic heirs, Nietzsche and Heidegger. We contend that Strauss mistakenly accepts the contemporary era as the world that Hegel projected as perfectly ethical. Instead, agreeing with Pippin, who says that Hegel's "ideal of freedom should not be rejected but properly realized," we assert that the contemporary world as viewed by Strauss reveals elements of Hegel's account of morality and is not fully revelatory of what Hegel believes is a truly ethical life.[46]

Hegel's account of the insufficiency of morality is most clearly revealed by its eventual negation. In abstract right one commits crimes; in the realm of morality one becomes evil. In the first, the individual infringes on the objective law that he assumed was governing his activities; in the latter, he is judged no longer by any objective standard, but rather by the court of conscience, the same court that allows his activities to flourish in the first place.

As noted, morality grows out of the conscious dissatisfaction of an objective law that does not account for the inner determination of its agents. This deficiency explains the crimes of abstract right. In the stage of morality, individual subjectivity becomes all-important. However, in retreating from the empty and unfeeling laws of objectivity, the moral person gives himself over to the contingencies of his own ends and desires without any standard for governing these except his autonomy. While even assuming the best of intentions, such as the welfare of all, or the good in and of itself, such a person may as easily commit acts of evil as acts of good: "The right to recognize nothing that I do not perceive as rational is the highest right of the subject, but by virtue of its subjective determination, it is at the same time *formal*. . . . Because of its formal determination, insight is equally capable of being *true* and of being mere *opinion* and *error*."[47] While one may understand that one *ought* to do good things, this *ought* is given content by oneself, and one's understanding of the good is often determined by mitigating factors such as one's particular tastes and interests or one's particular education. As a result, there is no necessary correlation between what one person intends and wills as the good, and an actually good outcome.

Even prior to the full discussion of evil, we see the difficulty of the moral will which seeks the welfare of itself and others regardless of whether this welfare is right or just. While Hegel contends that ultimately seeking the satisfaction of one's personal welfare and the welfare of others is rational, without an objective account of why this is rational and how it relates to the fulfillment of self-consciousness or real freedom, the moral person posits welfare as an appropriate end in and of itself. When one views the contemporary world with the eyes of Strauss, the moral position that Hegel describes dominates our political discourse. In Aristotelian language, we are more concerned with mere life than we are with living well.[48] The private individual is increasingly concerned with the satisfaction, health, and safety of his body, while those who are more socially conscious think of the physical well-being of fellow citizens and seek increasingly fulsome ways to secure welfare nets.

Hegel argues that an individual's rational capacity places an obligation on him to make correct judgments. It is a person's responsibility, insofar as his essence is self-consciousness, to be correct. Hegel says:

> What constitutes right and duty, as the rationality in and for itself of the will's determinations, is essentially neither the *particular* property of an individual, nor is its *form* that of feeling or any other individual – i.e., sensuous – kind of knowledge, but essentially that of *universal determinations of thought*, i.e., the form of *laws* and *principles*. The conscience is therefore subject to the judgment as to its *truth* or falsity.[49]

And "Where all previously valid determinations have vanished and the will is in a state of pure inwardness, the self-consciousness is capable of making into its principle, either *the universal in and for itself*, or the *arbitrariness* of its *own particularity*."[50] According to Hegel, evil occurs not only when a person intentionally does something he knows is wrong, but also anytime he mistakenly wills his own particularity as though it were the universal, even if, in doing this, he is certain that he is correct. Just as Aristotle says that it is a person's responsibility to know the objective end he should seek in his activity, so Hegel indicates that insofar as one is capable of distinguishing between right and wrong, he has an obligation to do so.[51] This is particularly true in the stage of morality, where people have made the capacity to individually determine benchmarks of right and wrong their sole intent.

As is clear through our discussion of ancient Greece, we know that the development of morality, and subsequently evil acts, can happen at any time. However, Hegel indicates that morality will be a more prevalent ethical stage after the advent of Christianity for two reasons. First, in Christ and through the Bible, the divine nature is revealed, and human beings are given the means by which they might know their true end. Further, the revelation of God as a particular person, and the fundamental equality of human beings that emerges from the Christian position, highlight the essential nature of subjectivity.[52]

While Hegel pinpoints Rousseau and, particularly, Kant as providing the philosophic foundation for morality, it is not difficult to see how the philosophy of Nietzsche and Heidegger, for example, also find a home in this broader class.[53] Indeed, Hegel would presumably argue that nihilism and existentialism are the logical ends of this particular train of thought.

As noted, Hegel indicates that the great problem of Kant's moral position is that it is impossible to only will what one would have everyone else universally will, when *what* one ought to will has not yet been determined. Further, Kant's epistemology makes discerning these objective principles impossible, for while one can believe that such principles exist, one can never have knowledge of their reality. Morally, the individual compensates for the loss of an objective knowledge of the universal by attempting to imitate its existence through a generalization of will. However, without an actual objective principle upon which to rest one's subjective judgments, it becomes possible to rationalize any end as just. As Hegel says:

> if we demand of a principle that it should also serve as the determinant of universal legislation, this presupposes that it already has content; and if this content were present, it would be easy to apply the principle. But in this case, the principle itself is not yet available, and the criterion that there should be no contradiction is non-productive—for where there is nothing, there can be no contradiction either.[54]

If, as Hegel suggests, this account of moral philosophy leaves the determination of the will entirely to the contingency of the subjective individual, then the next logical step would be clarification of this point, such as we see in much postmodern political thought.

The authentic human, as described by Nietzsche and Heidegger, embraces the absolute subjectivity implied in Kant's position. Recognizing that there can be no universal principles upon which they might base their activities, individuals will themselves as that universal. Hegel seemingly describes exactly this position when he notes, "since such philosophizing maintains that the knowledge of truth is an empty vanity which transcends the sphere of cognition, and that the latter is mere semblance, it must immediately make this very semblance its principle as far as action is concerned, and thereby equate the ethical with the *distinctive* outlook of the individual and his *particular conviction*."[55] Rather than being the logical successors of Hegel, as Strauss suggests, it seems that Nietzsche and Heidegger are more obviously the result of Kant's epistemological and moral position. This seems to be particularly the case when one realizes what is common in the philosophy of Kant, Nietzsche, and Heidegger: the incapacity to know any objective determining principle. This is the exact point that Hegel is criticizing and responding to in his account of the insufficiency of moral life. As a result, Hegel's philosophy is categorically distinct from these three. Hegel ends the discussion of morality describing the final attitude of its agents, saying "objective goodness is merely something constructed by my conviction, sustained by me alone, and that I, as lord and master, can make it come and go [as I please]. As soon as I relate myself to something objective, it ceases to exist for me, and so I am poised above an immense void, conjuring up shapes and destroying them."[56]

While Strauss sees the barbarism of the twentieth century as an indication that Hegel's progressive account of history is obviously false, Hegel's argument instead points to the understanding that evil results from the moral position posited by Romantic philosophers and this is further "clarified" by philosophers following Hegel. Regardless of whether Hegel is correct to suggest that this is the ethical position of Kant, it is clear that it is a position that Hegel explicitly rejects and one that he believes his philosophy ultimately transcends. In the next chapter, we will make the case that there are indications in the contemporary world that suggest that Hegel's latter point is correct. Hegel further suggests that the prevalence of what one might understand as evil may be the means by which humans, more broadly, or the world-historical individual, more specifically, recognize the insufficiency of this philosophic and moral position and finally begin to make the transition to ethical life. For, Hegel tells us, morality and its outcome in evil are not merely philosophic speculations, but rather, insofar as the truth is dialectically engaged with social and political phenomena, these truths find an outlet in human activity: "The degradation into which philosophy has thus sunk seems at first glance, in the eyes of the world, an utterly indifferent happening which has affected only the idle talk of academics; but such a view necessarily becomes part of our view of ethics . . . and only then do the implications of these views become apparent in and for [the realm of] actuality."[57] The logical implication of the system of morality results, as Hegel tells us, in evil and such evil, when enacted in the world, should force at least some human beings to recognize that the world lacks the recognition of true objective standards and is not as rationally satisfying as may have been previously thought. Strauss, perhaps unwittingly, takes up the role of Hegel's world-historical individual in his attempt to return contemporary thought and ethics to an objective grounding.

Ironically, one can see this element of Strauss's criticism against Hegel as fulfilling part of Hegel's argument. Unfortunately, rather than projecting a new ethical life, wherein the gains made by human subjectivity might be reconciled with the objective good, Strauss, instead, seeks to return human beings, at least philosophically, to ancient Greece. As described earlier, however, philosophy will always be in tension with the Greek world because the development of philosophy requires recognizing the value of independent human thought or human subjectivity. It is the philosophic independence of Socrates that results in the destruction of the objective Greek order. On this basis, we might see more clearly why it is that Strauss believes that philosophy will always be in conflict with one's political life. The Greek political order that Strauss seemingly prefers cannot withstand the strength of individual thought.

We might thus recall that Hegel identifies the ethical attitude of Socrates as belonging to the sphere of morality. Socrates, unlike other Athenians, is not content to unconsciously accept the bounds of tradition or biology; instead, as a moral being, he seeks to subjectively understand the good and wills only what he so understands. Hegel argues that the moral position is the appropriate one for Socrates to take because the objective moral around him had "fallen into ruin. He evaporated the existing world and retreated into himself in search of the right and the good."[58] Hegel's point here seems to be to critique those of his own age, who, refusing to recognize the rationality of the actual external world in which they live, prefer instead their own particular and subjective judgments. In this we might also see a critique of the reactionary conservative movement that is often, rightly or wrongly, associated with Strauss. While Strauss rejects the emphasis on pure subjectivity that morality seems to inspire, Hegel's description of morality also encompasses those who, in seeking to do duty for duty's sake, judge all other motivations as self-interested and tainted. Moyar notes that Hegel's critique of morality includes the "self-righteous judge" who accepts as legitimate only the rule of pure reason, assuming that they are in a position to determine what is rational.[59]

As we have seen, Hegel argues that political orders are the manifestation of a community's understanding of its nature and of the nature of spirit. While at any given moment such communities may fall short of a complete account, insofar as they are at all stable, they do project some element of the truth. Denying this is to project one's own particular judgment over the manifest truth of an age. While Hegel argues that at times this kind of judgment is appropriate, he cautions us against making it without due cause, saying, "Only in ages when the actual world is a hollow spiritless, and unsettled existence, may the individual be permitted to flee from actuality and retreat into his inner life," for "everything which we recognize as right or duty can be shown to be null and void, limited and in no way absolute."[60] Hegel's point is that given the particular contingent nature of any actual political community, one can always find cause for dissatisfaction. However, in withdrawing from the world in favor of one's particular determinations, one runs the risk of overlooking what is actually rational in favor of one's subjective, particular, and perhaps contingent preferences.

The ancient world that Strauss seeks, if only philosophically, is a world that is incapable of maintaining itself; the life of virtue and ultimately the philosophy that develops within it, is the cause of its own destruction. Strauss himself seems to recognize this. Hegel, however, points to a more complete vision of human possibility, saying:

> This Greek morality, though extremely beautiful, attractive and interesting in its manifestation, is not the highest point of view for Spiritual self-consciousness. It wants the form of Infinity, the reflection of thought within itself, the emancipation from the Natural element—(the Sensuous that lurks in the character of Beauty and Divinity [as comprehended by the Greeks])—and from that immediacy, [that undeveloped simplicity,] which attaches to their ethics. Self-Comprehension on the part of Thought is wanting—illimitable Self-Consciousness—demanding, that what is regarded as Right and Morality should have its confirmation in myself—from the testimony of my own Spirit; that the Beautiful (the Idea as manifested in sensuous contemplation or conception) may also become the True—an inner, supersenusous world.[61]

The development of morality points to the inward sublation of the objective forms of abstract right. Moral individuals, such as Socrates, are not content to be determined by merely external laws; instead they seek to understand the nature of right themselves. In ethical life the external world is reclaimed as moral individuals posit the grounds of their rational judgment in objective institutions and laws thereby overcoming the pure subjectivity and potential contingency of morality. In the following chapter, we will seek to demonstrate that the contemporary era, and the manifold development of individual particularity and thought that it encourages, is capable of promoting and supporting the objective truth and ethical good that Strauss's philosophy seeks.

NOTES

1. Pangle, *Leo Strauss: An Introduction to His Thought and Intellectual Legacy*, 79. See also, Bloom, *The Closing of the American Mind*.
2. For alternative accounts, please see, Pippin, *Modernism as a Philosophic Problem*, 160–79.
3. Hegel, *Elements of the Philosophy of Right*, sect. 62.
4. Doull, "Hegel on the English Reform Bill," 43–54.
5. Hegel, *Phenomenology*, sect. 442.
6. Ibid., sect. 441 and Hegel, *The Philosophy of History*, 267.
7. Hegel, *The Philosophy of History*, 223.
8. Hegel, *Phenomenology of Spirit*, sect. 457–59.
9. Plato, *The Republic*, 331, d–e.
10. Hegel, *Elements of the Philosophy of Right*, sect. 166.
11. Hegel, *The Philosophy of History*, 252.
12. Hegel, *Phenomenology of Spirit*, sect. 465.
13. Hegel, *The Philosophy of History*, 267.
14. Strauss, "On Classical Political Philosophy," 74–75.
15. Strauss, "Natural Right and the Distinction Between Facts and Values," 82.
16. Hegel, *The Philosophy of History*, 267.
17. Ibid., 253, 267–68.
18. Ibid., 269.
19. Ibid., 265.
20. Thucydides, *The History of the Peloponnesian War*, Book 5, 84–116.
21. Hegel, *The Philosophy of History*, 269.
22. Hegel, *Phenomenology of Spirit*, sect. 480.
23. Hegel, *Elements of the Philosophy of Right*, sect. 40, and Hegel, *Phenomenology of Spirit*, sect. 477–80.
24. Hegel, *Elements of the Philosophy of Right*, sect. 138 and sect. 138 add.
25. Ibid., sect. 32. See Franco, *Hegel's Philosophy of Freedom*, 191.
26. Strauss, Papers [Box 9, Folder 2], Special Collections Research Center, University of Chicago Library.
27. Leo Strauss, "Seminar in Political Philosophy: Hegel's *The Philosophy of History*" (lecture, The Leo Strauss Centre, leostrausscenter.uchicago.edu, January 12, 1965).
28. Hegel, *The Philosophy of History*, 21.
29. Ibid.
30. Ibid., sect. 37 and sect. 37 add.
31. Ibid., sect. 39.
32. Ibid., sect. 40 & 43.
33. Ibid., sect. 41 add. See Locke, *Two Treatises of Government*, II, 123, 15. See Allen W. Wood, *Hegel's Ethical Thought*, 95-6.
34. Hegel, *Elements of the Philosophy of Right*, sect. 81.
35. Ibid., sect. 104.
36. Ibid., sect. 129.
37. Ibid., 106.
38. Franco, *Hegel's Philosophy of Freedom*, 209.

39. Ibid., sect. 121.
40. Ibid., sect. 123.
41. Ibid., sect. 126.
42. Ibid., sect. 131.
43. Ibid., sect. 132.
44. Ibid., sect. 135.
45. Ibid., sect. 137.
46. Pippin, *The Persistence of Subjectivity*, 2.
47. Hegel, *Elements of the Philosophy of Right*, sect. 132.
48. Aristotle, *Politics*, 1252b, 26–29.
49. Ibid., sect. 137
50. Ibid., sect.139. Franco further posits that this responsibility to know and will what is universally true is also inherent in Hegel's earlier account intention. See Franco, *Hegel's Philosophy of Freedom*, 209–10.
51. Aristotle, *Nicomachean Ethics*, 1110b, 25–30.
52. Aesthetically, Hegel refers to the entire modern period, from the advent of Christianity to the contemporary period as Romantic.
53. For example, see Hegel, *Elements of the Philosophy of Right*, 29, 135A.
54. Hegel, *Elements of the Philosophy of Right*, sect. 135 add.
55. Ibid., sect. 140.
56. Ibid., sect. 140 add.
57. Ibid., sect. 140.
58. Ibid., 138A
59. Moyar, *Hegel's Conscience*, 72–74.
60. Ibid.
61. Hegel, *The Philosophy of History*, 264–65.

FIVE

Ethical Realities

The central signifier for Strauss and Straussians of the flaws of modernity is that in exchanging virtue for freedom as the guiding principle of society, modernity has produced a world of last men, a place of "men without chests."[1] This view is the flashpoint for the most spirited criticisms of the Straussian political philosophy. To many contemporary critics, some more inclined to hyperbole than others, Strauss's argument smacks of elitism, anti-democratic sentiments, and even fascism.[2] To claim that by granting freedom and equality to all people, modernity thereby precludes the possibility of excellence seems to belong to the most reactionary and offensive conservativism. Strauss was certainly aware of the contrarian nature of his position and how repugnant it would be to contemporary sensibilities. We are of the opinion that a good number of Strauss's critics in this regard have ventured well beyond what the evidence would support. It may be that a habitual reaction against any hint of elitist thought prevents some from acknowledging the simple truth of many of Strauss's observations about the shallowness of much of contemporary civic life and culture.

Further, we have argued that the kind of freedom Strauss condemned would have been similarly condemned by Hegel. Our claim is that Strauss attaches the label of relativist to Hegel unfairly. Further, we argue that Hegel's advocacy for subjectivity was only in relation to the presence of the objective good. Rather than denying the possibility of nobility, Hegel sought to show that the pursuit of the good was more universally possible within his ethical state, and that it is only within a free society that human beings in general can attain the best life. Hegel was, like Strauss, aware of the destructive aspects of a free subjectivity for human beings not conditioned by rational institutions.

While no one could plausibly argue that we live in a completely ethical society, there is evidence to suggest that contemporary liberal democracies have made substantial progress towards achieving such a societal form. The record of modern barbarism, from the several instances of genocide in the twentieth century, to the continued existence of child slavery, and widespread sexual exploitation of women, tolerated if not facilitated by democratic societies, would argue against signs of ethical progress. Popular culture in North America and Europe is often violent, seldom thoughtful, and primarily driven less by aesthetic aspirations than by crude economic calculation. Neither communism nor capitalism nor some combination of these, in practice, has demonstrated itself to be an entirely rational (let alone ethical) economic system. This, however, is only one side of the evidence.

In most modern societies, recognition of the rights of the individual is assumed. The constitutions of modern liberal democracies not only generally recognize the dignity of all citizens, but also reflect aspirations toward justice as well as freedom. The U.S. Constitution, for example, affirms not simply private freedom, but also a vision of a common social order: "We the People of the United States, in Order to form a more perfect Union, establish Justice, insure domestic Tranquillity, provide for the common defence, promote the general Welfare, and secure the Blessings of Liberty to ourselves and our Posterity, do ordain and establish this Constitution for the United States of America." A critic might observe that there is a certain Hobbesian reductionism present in this description of the Union's purpose. The Declaration of Independence scarcely asserts more: "We hold these truths to be self-evident, that all men are created equal, that they are endowed by their Creator with certain unalienable Rights, that among these are Life, Liberty and the pursuit of Happiness.—That to secure these rights, Governments are instituted among Men, deriving their just powers from the consent of the governed." And yet, from these seeds, the United States has developed a remarkable record of social progress. In asserting that government derives its powers from the consent of the governed there is affirmed a confidence that rational people, within the structures of modern political institutions, will direct their wills towards the common good. In his Second Inaugural address, Lincoln declared:

> Fondly do we hope, fervently do we pray, that this mighty scourge of war may speedily pass away. Yet, if God wills that it continue until all the wealth piled by the bondsman's two hundred and fifty years of unrequited toil shall be sunk, and until every drop of blood drawn with the lash shall be paid by another drawn with the sword, as was said three thousand years ago, so still it must be said "the judgments of the Lord are true and righteous altogether.

This uniting of the free will of a people with an objective, or divine, good is not unique to the American form of liberal democracy, even if it is more often explicitly expressed there.

A more recent liberal constitution is that of Canada. The same principles apply, although tailored to the particular contingencies of the Canadian historical context. As with American legal documents, individual liberties are linked to an objective, eternal principle:

> Whereas Canada is founded upon the principles that recognize the supremacy of God and the rule of law. . . . The Canadian Charter of Rights and Freedoms guarantees the rights and freedoms set out in it subject only to such reasonable limits prescribed by law as can be demonstrably justified in a free and democratic society. Everyone has the following fundamental freedoms: (a) freedom of conscience and religion; (b) freedom of thought, belief, opinion and expression, including freedom of the press and other means of communication; (c) freedom of peaceful assembly; and (d) freedom of association.

While fundamentally a statement of liberalism, the practical working-out of these constitutional principles has resulted in a weighing of private and public goods for Canada and other liberal democracies. The achieved effect has been the attainment of a balance recognized, for the most part, by all citizens.

One might argue that little is proven when speaking in such broad and theoretical strokes. Yet, we believe that there is more particular and practical evidence of ethical life in the contemporary world. Hegel identifies three spheres as essential to the development of ethical citizens: the family, civil society, and the state. Each of these, he argues, takes up and develops an essential element of human life such that one would be satisfied within the modern political order and also a willing and thoughtful contributor to the same. While each of these spheres are prominent in contemporary western societies, developments in each go well beyond what Hegel envisioned. These same developments have also drawn heavy criticism from conservative circles, both political and scholarly. Yet as Moyar notes, "It is very easy to lament the loss of unity from early days gone by, when everyone knew what was right and did it."[3] Yet this "right" behavior did not include the emancipation of women, full civil rights for African Americans, or equal rights for the LGBTQ community. Hegel argues that human life is the free and objective manifestation of the essence of spirit. Our social and political orders exist because as citizens we broadly accept that they are reasonable and do a satisfactory job of fulfilling their designed ends. It is not our argument, nor Hegel's position, that everything is rational. The rationality of contemporary developments depends, in this account, on their further mediating or reconciling the particular wills of individuals with the rational and objective ends of the wider political community. In the following sections, we will look at examples of development, often controversial, in each sphere of Hegel's ethical community, and seek to demonstrate how modernity is on a path to a greater ethical ground because of such changes.

THE MODERN FAMILY

The family, Hegel remarks, is the stage of immediate ethical activity.[4] Love serves as the foundation of familial relationships and results in individuals who act naturally for the sake of the whole and, in so doing, achieve happiness. Simply put, one seeks the happiness of the beloved because this is the means to one's own happiness. In a properly functioning family, Hegel's ethical state is prefigured in its immediate and natural form. While citizens of the political community must work to understand their place within the whole, members of a family find their places naturally and are readily able to sacrifice themselves for each other because, in so doing, they find satisfaction.

The nature and shape of the family has been significantly transformed since Hegel's age and is the subject of much controversy and debate. Modernity, Hegel tells us, is characterized by its emphasis on subjectivity and the family, even his own era, was not an exception to this rule. He critically notes, "In modern times . . . the subjective origin [of marriage], the *state of being in love*, is regarded as the only important factor. Here, it is imagined that each must wait until his hour has struck, and that one can give one's love only to a specific individual."[5] The Romantic Movement had such a profound effect on Hegel's age and it still colors at least the western world's view of love and marriage. With the development of reproductive technologies, and the growing social and political acceptance of same sex marriage, it is clear that the satisfaction of individual subjective preferences has become a defining characteristic of modern family life. On this, contemporary liberals and conservatives would probably agree, even though they would clearly differ on the merits of this new reality.

Many conservatives argue that these developments point to a destruction of the family, and undermine moral and ethical development in individuals. Current transformations of the family, many argue, show that the foundation of the contemporary order is under attack. Alternatively, we believe that many contemporary reformulations of the family are indicative of the creation of stronger families and illustrate the essential role that families continue to play in society. These developments result in a more solid basis for social and political communities. The advent of same sex marriages is one example of a transformation that, we believe, is in accordance with the logic of Hegel's argument, even if it is a development that Hegel did not conceive of or predict. The legalization of gay marriage is evidence of the yearning to incorporate subjectively founded relationships within rational institutions and furthers Hegel's argument that ethical life mediates the particularity of desire within the boundaries of a developed and rational political life.

Marriage, Hegel says, while springing from emotion and desire, transcends these purely contingent elements and raises them to the level appropriate for a rational institution. By means of the wedding ceremony and the commitment that embarking on married life entails, individuals who marry are asked to consciously consider the nature of their emotions and their capacity for commitment. Hegel notes that in marriage, "the natural drive is reduced to the modality of a moment of nature which is destined to be extinguished in its very satisfaction, while the spiritual bond asserts *its rights* as the substantial factor . . . as indissoluble *in itself* an exalted above the contingency of the passions and of particular transient caprice."[6] The mediation of the institution of marriage has the effect, Hegel writes, of sublating the contingent and, often, arbitrary element of desire within a rational form.

In other words, individuals who choose to get married, excepting the most cynical of people, intend their marriages to last their lifetime. They consciously limit any further amorous relationships to this one person and indicate that this is a choice that can be reasonably sustained. In the act of marriage, individuals are brought to seek a larger good than merely their own personal fulfillment, for now they must consider the happiness of at least one other person. The marriage ceremony further mediates the particularity of desires, for through this external and formal rite, individuals declare the ethical nature of their intentions. What may have been only inwardly intended is thereby made objective to participants. Hegel describes the ethical necessity of marriage, saying, "It is accordingly only after this ceremony has *first taken place*, as the completion of the *substantial* [aspect of marriage] by means of the *sign*—i.e., by means of language as the most spiritual existence of the spiritual—that this bond has been ethically constituted."[7] Marriage, Hegel argues, is neither merely a contract nor just the fulfillment of one's romantic inclinations, but rather the ethical basis of the family, and, as such, the root of all other ethical determinations.

Of course, this is not to deny the obvious truth that many couples take marriage lightly or thoughtlessly rush into bad matches because of the immediacy of a desire or an intention that quickly fades without any rational foundation to sustain it. There are, and will always be, these types of marriages—among both straight and gay couples. Yet, it would be difficult to demonstrate, we believe, that there will be a greater number of instances of thoughtless and desire-driven gay marriages than there have been and will be among straight couples. Certainly, it would be unfair, if even possible, to seek statistics on the number of successful gay and straight marriages in the current timeframe as proof. Only recently given the right to marry, and then only in some places, it can be expected that some gay marriages are political acts or gestures, rather than consummations of ethical love. However, assuming that these political rights last and are extended, in time we would expect to discover that the number of successful gay marriages will be proportionate to the number of successful straight marriages. Similarly, the reasons for failed marriages will be as complicated and varied in both groups. We suggest that greater acceptance of same sex unions offers a greater scope for the inclusion of diverse relationships within the rational institution of marriage and the greater opportunity of ordering individual desires.

How can it be detrimental to the ethical state that Hegel describes, to recognize, incorporate, and satisfy the need for love among all members of a political community? Love, Hegel tells us, is a kind of paradox. The individual loses himself in it, only to find himself more sufficiently than before.[8] This paradox is both immediate and natural, and is a necessary basis for the development of ethical life in the further community, both civil and political. In loving someone else, a person becomes habituated to seeing himself in relationship to others and comes naturally to understand his nature as a social creature. His happiness is dependent upon the well-being and happiness of the people he loves and, more broadly, the well-being of the political communities he inhabits. Clearly, adoption and the use of the same reproductive and social innovations (e.g., surrogate mothers and fathers) employed by opposite-sex couples make possible for same sex couples the opportunity to raise and nurture children. The social role that marriage plays in civil society can be performed by same sex couples as well as by opposite-sex couples, as experience is demonstrating in those jurisdictions where same sex marriage is allowed.

It would be no surprise to Plato or Aristotle that some people are attracted to members of the same sex. It is strange that it is such a revelation to so many moderns who would consider themselves enlightened. It is somewhat like being surprised that some men are bald and some have hair and then making a moral determination on these grounds.[9] However, as Plato knew, the above analogy is too superficial. Having hair or not is irrelevant in the formation of ethically conscious individuals. Experiencing reciprocated love, in a stable and formally recognized relationship, alternatively, is essential to both individual happiness and social stability. To deny this possibility to a significant segment of any population is detrimental not only to the individuals involved, but to the wider community in general.

As Hegel fully understood, individuals who are forced to deny some element of their natures because society refuses their rational incorporation cannot be truly ethical members of that community. Members of the LGBTQ community forced into straight relationships for the sake of satisfying conventional norms or even laws are presumably not only unhappy, but in all likelihood they also come to resent their partners, children, and the institutions that forced them together. Perceiving that these communities do not satisfy their own interests, it is improbable that they will make the ends of these communities their own. As a result, these families will often fail to create the kind of reciprocal recognition that is required for true participation in broader ethical communities. Not given a rational way to satisfy their interests, people in these circumstances will find irrational opportunities for satisfaction and these will undoubtedly be to the detriment of the communities in which they participate. When a wife resents her husband because he is male, she will find other things about him that she can legally and appropriately resent. Husbands, wives, and children, learning to satisfy themselves at the cost of each other, will carry these same habits into their civil and political communities. On the other hand, it is also the case that like any other rational individuals, LGBTQ people as well as straight can and do achieve an ethical habituation from participating in reciprocal relationships that are freely chosen and desired. The contingency of attraction has no bearing on the rational nature of those who love.

This argument is consistent with Hegel's Christianity, which has love as its basis. In his lectures on the philosophy of religion, Hegel affirms two things. First, "[love is the] most outstanding and at the same time most comprehensive teaching of Christ." Second, the "moral imperative" for Christianity is love, "not what is legally right, but the well-being of the other, hence a relationship to the particularity of the other."[10] The affirmation of these two principles leads to a remarkable passage of scriptural exegesis, wherein Hegel demonstrates that love allows for "a breaking away . . . from everything established."[11] The overturning of custom (e.g., Sabbath laws) is cited as an illustration of this breaking away, as seen in repeated episodes in the gospels.

Another consequence, according to Hegel, of the absolute primacy of love is radical equality: "Subjectivity has given up all external distinctions in this infinite value, distinctions of mastery, power, position, even of sex and wealth. Before God all human beings are equal."[12] Hegel recognizes immediately that in this "lies the possibility and the root of truly universal justice and the actualization of freedom." In the same passage he provides an example of the sexual freedom of women.

One might note that this argument is in contrast to what Hegel explicitly says about marriage as a union of the "natural determinacy of the two sexes."[13] In his account of traditional marriage, Hegel argues that differences between men and women are ethically significant, such that men, capable of more objective rationality, while women, predominantly defined by feelings, are more fully defined by spirit's particularity. On these grounds, Hegel argues that marriage between the two sexes reconciles these moments. In an immediate way, we are supposed to see the mediation that is more consciously and rationally achieved within the state occur within a marriage. Several scholars have argued that this element of Hegel's position runs counter to much of what he indicates about the nature of women and the roles that they have to perform in Hegel's ethical community as well as to the logic of his overall argument.[14] In an ethical family, individuals find satisfaction for their most immediate and natural desires in such a way that these desires are shown as commensurate with a more universal and rational end. Recognition of the full equality of the sexes does not have the effect of preventing this from happening. Having been granted civil and political equality, both men and women continue to be good spouses and good parents.

If we accept the argument that the physical difference of the sexes does not correspond to a necessary distinction between the nature of self-consciousness achieved by each and to an ethical significance, then in terms of Hegel's logic, we should also recognize that same sex marriages could fulfill the same ethical role as marriages between couples of different sexes. In support of this argument, Neuhouser writes, "Contrary to what contemporary advocates of 'family values' proclaim, same-sex marriages represent not the demise of the family, but a creative reconfiguration of it, one that enhances the family's ability to reproduce itself by making it less restrictive without compromising its ethical significance."[15] In describing traditional marriages, Hegel notes that the ethical nature of the union is such that it mediates the natural biological differences of the sexes. In this instance, the particular nature of women, as described by Hegel, complements and is complemented by, the nature of men. Needless to say, biological differences between the sexes would not be the only natural or particular difference between individuals in a marriage. As individuals, each with specific talents and desires, all partners in marriage, regardless of their sex, find ways that their particular natures are enhanced by and enhance the individuality of their spouses. Biology might be the most obvious way that the particular nature of an individual is mediated and made ethical by the institution of marriage, but it certainly is not the only conceivable natural difference that finds rational mediation in marriages and families.

Nonetheless, Hegel argues that the differences between the sexes play a more necessarily obvious function in the development of families, for marriages are given an objective presence in the world through reproduction and the raising of children. Children become the manifest means by which parents recognize the ethical significance of their union.[16] Further, in willing the good of a child, parents are brought to recognize their own fulfillment in an objective other that stands in a more remote relationship to them than does their partner. The ethical significance of children in a marriage is important.

Hegel's argument, however, cannot require all people to participate in a traditional marriage and have children in the traditional way in order to be ethical. For any number of reasons, individuals may choose not to or be unable to participate in these relationships and for just as many different reasons they may be better off not doing so. There is no reason to think that a single individual cannot find other means of participating in an ethical community, or that married couples that do not have children are incapable of being fully functioning members of an ethical state.[17] Moreover, technological advances as well as the possibility of adoption make it possible for otherwise childless same-sex couples, as well as opposite-sex couples to be parents. While there is perhaps the argument that the bond between a biological parent and child is more immediate, for the love between a parent and child to be ethical, it must extend beyond a biological connection. Certainly parents and adopted children form bonds of love that are enduring and that result in ethical families and ethical citizens. There is no objective reason to think that same-sex couples will be any less capable of loving and educating children than couples of opposite sexes.

Many developments in contemporary society were not on the immediate political horizon during Hegel's time. Nevertheless, the full emancipation of women, the abolition of slavery, the development of social welfare, among other social changes, were either foreseen by Hegel (and many others) or could be extrapolated from his thought. In the same way, the extension of equal rights to LGBTQ citizens is, at the least, not inconsistent with Hegel's argument about equality and freedom. As we have suggested, the double imperatives of including all forms of human subjectivity in relationship to the objective good and the recognition of the radical equality of all people require the emancipation of the LGBTQ community. For their relationships to be denied institutional recognition, and full participation in society, is to thwart both principles.

CIVIL SOCIETY

While the family represents the Hegelian self-consciousness in an immediate form, it is in civil society that Hegel believes human subjectivity is explicitly illuminated. Members of a family naturally see their ends as dependent upon, and entwined with the well-being of the family itself. The habituation for ethical life that takes place here is unconscious and individual subjectivity is sublimated to the good of the whole, seemingly without tension or thought. Yet, to be perfectly self-conscious and ethical, individuals must fully understand and participate in their particularity. Civil society is the realm where individuals freely express and satisfy their subjective natures. While civil society, as Hegel speaks of it, is primarily an economic entity, having its expression in what he calls the *Korporation*, other elements of society are also involved, including the justice system and public education. Although "Corporations," as Hegel defined them, were not to emerge as the social force he envisaged, other elements of his account of civil society are nonetheless relevant.

Civil society is the realm of selfish diversity in all of its minute detail.[18] It is also the realm, however, where individuals are forced to see the necessary relationship among their most particular and selfish desires, the universality of their rational capacity, and that of the community in which they participate. In this, civil society performs a mediating function between the particularity of the family and the rational order of the state. For Hegel, even the capacity to multiply one's needs and desires to seemingly infinite proportions is itself a sign that one is a rational and universal being.[19] Moreover, in seeking to satisfy their interests, people recognize their need for others even if, at this stage, the other is merely a means to their own fulfillment: "in the very act of developing itself . . . the principle of particularity passes over into *universality*, and only in the latter does it have its truth and its right to positive actuality. This unity is not that of ethical identity . . . it is present not as freed, but as . . . *necessity*."[20] This moment, of seeing a necessary, if yet undesired, relationship between one's particularity and the universal is the second stage of an education of a truly ethical being.

In the family, we immediately mimic the ethical activity of the state and are unconsciously brought to see our ends as identical to those of the larger whole. The ethical life of the state, however, is not one that is easily achieved. While it is perhaps natural to equate one's interests with those of the people one loves, it is less likely that an individual will see this connection between himself and unknown numbers of fellow citizens, let alone with the often faceless institutions of the state. Achieving an ethical relationship to a political community requires an education. Integral to this education is the freedom granted in civil society for the fulfillment of subjective interests, whether it is in matters of employment or entertainment. Hegel writes, "In this situation, the interest of the Idea, which is not present in the consciousness of . . . members of civil society . . . is the *process* whereby their individuality and naturalness are raised by natural necessity and by their arbitrary needs, *to formal freedom* and formal *universality of knowledge and volition*, and subjectivity is educated in the process."[21] It is precisely this "education of subjectivity" that is often overlooked by contemporary conservative critics of Hegel. We might compare Hegel's position to Augustine's. Augustine wrote of the *ordo amoris*, whereby a person's various loves are directed to their proper end in God.[22] In this account subjective desires are trained, step by step, to ascend towards the highest objective end. For Hegel, a more complete exploration of human subjectivity is envisaged. Rather than overcoming inferior objects in the ascent to God, the form of modern society, reflecting the full social explication of the Christian religion (as yet not realized in Augustine's thought or society), accommodates our subjective freedom more completely in the universal.

The individual enters civil society seeking only to fulfill his particular desires. However, in order to do so, he realizes that he must conform to and participate in the larger community. Moreover, he may also realize that his initial interests have to be transformed or even curtailed if he is to enjoy any part of them. This seemingly external process whereby one is forced to conform to the universal norms of society has an internal educational benefit. The individual realizes the necessary relationship between his desires and those of society as a whole. While not yet an ethical individual, he thereby achieves the kind of enlightened self-interest described by Tocqueville.[23] For Hegel, however, there is a stage beyond enlightened self-interest operating in civil society:

> The selfish end in its actualization, conditioned in this way by universality, establishes a system of all-round interdependence, so that the subsistence and welfare of the individual and his rightful existence are interwoven with, and grounded on, the subsistence, welfare, and rights of all, and have actuality and security only in this context.[24]

An individual who achieves enlightened self-interest is able to clearly see how the fulfillment of his particular desires depends on his participation in the common good. Hegel's ethical civil society ultimately does not allow for a ready division between personal interests and those of the whole. The interdependence between these presupposed binaries is such that they cannot be easily distinguished. The complex web of economic relationships, whether formally expressed through contracts or more casually exemplified through daily acts of exchange, have the necessary corollary of mutual recognition of persons and property. Rights, in turn, proceed from these foundational forms of recognition and, as we know, are continually developed to reflect changing aspects of the civil society that requires them in order to function.

Here we see an important distinction between Hegel and Strauss. Our argument is not that Strauss is simply an enemy of modernity as some have argued. Catherine and Michael Zuckert have responded clearly to many of the most egregious distortions of Leo Strauss's political thought.[25] Notwithstanding their well-supported demonstration that Strauss was a defender of liberal democracy, Strauss's defense stands on the vital caveat that this regime is only "the best possible under modern circumstances."[26] Of course, Hegel offers a less reserved support for modern liberalism. This unreserved liberalism is the point of difficulty for many on the right, including Strauss, as we have discussed earlier. Finding modern liberalism grounded in the passions, as opposed to the ancient grounding of human society in virtue, Hegel's liberalism is seen to abandon human nature's higher end. The proliferation of rights is pointed to as an indication of a climate of entitlement wherein individual expectations do not directly correlate with merit or activity. Francis Fukuyama, a Straussian, says, "Rights spring from an understanding of what man is, but if there is no argument on the nature of man, or a belief that such an understanding in principle is impossible, then any attempt to define rights or to prevent the creation of new and possibly spurious ones will be unavailing."[27] Hegel's position, however, is not that the passions, in finding their fulfillment in the modern regime, are intended to remain as the foundation of human life. Rather, the economic interests of civil society and the emphasis on rights move people from mere subjectivity to contributors of a recognizable objective order.

Civil society, in Hegel's account, is a fairly demanding taskmaster. While being the sphere for the satisfaction of desire, it is also the place where people encounter, and are habituated to, numerous obligations. Contracts, the law, education, and recognition of the rights of others all inexorably draw one's particularity into relation to the universal. The gradual acceptance of more expansive lists of human rights, beyond those applicable to the majority, are surely illustrative of a social attitude that is not merely rooted in individual selfishness, even if the impetus for "new rights" springs from particular desires. The multiplication of rights places more growing demands on civil and political institutions, and the objective order is transformed by the continued recognition of further elements of individual particularity. However, once rights are formally recognized, individuals living in these communities must respond accordingly. This is an important point when, in many instances, the right or freedom granted is not one that every individual will enjoy to the same extent. While ethical institutions are transformed by this movement, so too is the understanding of individual citizens.

The recognition of a diversity of rights within civil society is a completion of the Christian Idea in secular form. It is clear to any observer that the post-modern collapse of trust in institutions—religious, political, economic—has ushered in a period of significant instability in civil society. Yet, even amid a deeply polarized civic landscape, more rights are recognized, and rights that were novel a generation ago, are assumed today. For example, the rights of mentally and physically disabled people to receive accommodation by civic institutions would be questioned by few nowadays. Yet, less than fifty years ago, disabled citizens were often denied access to educational institutions, participation in the economy and a host of other freedoms. Despite the vacuity of much of contemporary popular culture, and the countless illustrations of an economic order that is exploitative and grounded in the lowest aspects of human nature, social progress in terms of the recognition of a common human worth continues. One might look to China, where the emergence of an economic middle class is producing necessarily a demand for greater freedom and the recognition of rights. A greater proportion of society, throughout any time in history, has access to civil liberties. In liberal democratic societies, as anticipated by Hegel, civil society is founded upon and engaged in promoting human beings as free. Hegel's account of civil society is not a narrow account of human freedom that debases people as passion-driven egotists. Rather, it is an aspirational account that seeks to model society such that the highest aspects of human nature may be enjoyed universally and not only be the pursuit of a fortunate few.

THE STATE

Hegel had both high and low expectations of the relationship between citizens and the state. As indicated previously, it is in relationship to the state that an individual can most completely experience self-consciousness and develop an ethical identity. While this might happen for some people some of the time, as we have argued, Hegel did not think that all people would achieve this level of ethical development. Nonetheless, we argue that the modern political world exceeds Hegel's expectations with respect to the development of ethical self-consciousness in contemporary political communities.

The state, in its ideal form, embodies the self-consciousness of its citizenry. In the form of its institutions and laws, it demonstrates rational universality. By means of differentiation within its structure, the state also embodies the particular in its necessary and rational form. While a citizen can achieve self-consciousness by being recognized and thus recognizing himself in the mind of another, so too, and perhaps even more fully, is self-consciousness achieved in light of a state that fully takes up his nature as its own. Hence, "it is only through being a member of the state that the individual . . . has objectivity, truth, and ethical life."[28] Hegel's further description of the state as the "march of God in the world" indicates the importance that Hegel places on the role of the state in fulfilling self-consciousness.[29] Through his participation in civil society, the individual learns the necessity of conforming elements of his will to the universal if he is to achieve any satisfaction; by means of his participation with the political community, the individual learns that his true satisfaction and freedom is the universal and he comes to desire its ends as his own.

Hegel tells us that this description of the state is not of any particular state, but rather of the state as Idea. Of actual states, Hegel notes that it is unlikely that any will completely achieve the rational form described in the *Elements of the Philosophy of Right*. He explains, "The state is not a work of art; it exists in the world, and hence in the sphere of arbitrariness, contingency, and error, and bad behaviour may disfigure it in many respects. But the ugliest man . . . is still a living human being; the affirmative aspect—life—survives in spite of such deficiencies, and it is with this affirmative aspect that we are here concerned."[30] Given the reality of how political communities operate in the world, Hegel is realistic about the possibilities of a perfectly ethical community. His point, instead, is only that insofar as a state is rational is it ethical.

When describing the ethical state, Hegel explains that its rationality does not depend on whether individuals recognize it as such or not.[31] Instead, he suggests, many citizens will not perceive the ethical nature of their relationship to the state. Indeed, when explaining the role played by the members of legislative assemblies, Hegel says that despite one's expectation that these delegates are beneficial because they know what is in the best interest of the people, it is exactly this that these members do not know: "To know what one wills . . . is the fruit of profound cognition and insight, and this is the very thing which 'the people' lack."[32] Hegel is not a naïve political idealist.

Setting aside what might be viewed, depending on one's perspective, as either Hegel's realism or pessimism, the overall current of his argument is that as modernity progresses states and presumably their citizens will become more ethical; we believe there is evidence of this development in the contemporary world. One of the greatest objections that one might point to in argument against a more ethical citizenry is the general political apathy that makes itself most prominently apparent during elections. In the western world, it seems that even the effort to vote is too much for many as turnout rates for federal elections in both Canada and the United States hover between 60 and 70 percent.[33] It could be difficult to argue that individuals desire the good of the state as their own, when they seemingly do not care who will govern it.

Turnout rates at elections are not, however, the only indicator of political engagement. Hegel argues that large states will, by their very nature, dissuade many people from voting on the grounds that any rational individual will be able to easily assess how little his vote is worth in such a context.[34] Nonetheless, several things should be noted with respect to voter turnout. First, we are assessing whether or not more people currently perceive a common commitment between themselves and their political organizations as a whole than in previous ages. Have the majority of people transcended the position that their relationship to the state is merely a contractual one whereby they pay taxes and in return the state protects their lives, liberty, and property? Are people now more willing and even desirous of having a state that looks to the advantage of the whole, even if it means greater sacrifices for the individual?

As evidence in favor of this proposition we might look to highly developed social and economic safety nets that exist in western nations and the difficulty with which any government proceeds when seeking to eliminate these benefits. Roosevelt articulated the positive support for this in his second inaugural address in 1937: "The test of our progress is not whether we add more to the abundance of those who have much; it is whether we provide enough for those who have too little." That this statement was not considered especially controversial at the time is a measure of the general acceptance of the principles of the New Deal, regardless of the subsequent imperfections in the application of FDR's vision. By 1971, even Richard Nixon could admit that he had become a Keynesian.

It is an unfortunate reality of most western nations that the majority of people who depend on the welfare state are, for a variety of reasons, without a voice in social debate. Instead, it is those who, most often, carry the tax burden for these programs that ensure they are maintained. It is presumably safe to say that the majority of people in the western world accept, in principle, that one role of the state is the protection of all individuals within it, although they may disagree about certain details as to how this is accomplished.[35]

As true as this may be, it is also important to note that Hegel does not emphasize the development of social and economic safety nets as the most important role of the ethical state. Instead, his focus is on the state in its capacity to develop a rational and self-conscious citizenry. Yet, he recognizes with great insight the problem of poverty for both individuals as well as the community as a whole. Hegel explains:

> [The poor person] is conscious of himself as an infinite, free being, and thus arises the demand that his external existence should correspond to this consciousness . . . [But] The poor man feels as if he were related to an arbitrary will, to human contingency . . . that he is put into this state of division through an arbitrary will. Self-consciousness appears driven to the point where it no longer has any rights, where freedom has no existence.[36]

Some would undoubtedly argue that the prominence of the current welfare state opposes the creation of rational and ethical citizens, creating instead a population that is dependent on the larger whole and unable to achieve the level of self-consciousness that Hegel describes.[37] While true perhaps in certain instances, this position has at least two flaws. First, it ignores the systemic and cultural causes of poverty and disengagement that for many blameless people are next to impossible to overcome on their own. Equal opportunity requires that everyone start at the same position regardless of where they then end up.[38] Second, such a position ascribes the worst to those who, for whatever reason, participate in social welfare programs, assuming that once they have received these benefits, they will be satisfied with them and will not seek to gain an independent life of their own. While this may be true of some, presumably it is not of all, and we believe most would agree that it is worth the cost of taking care of those who are unable to take care of themselves, thereby giving some the opportunity to enter what Hegel describes as a rational ethical life. Political apathy aside, there is some evidence that citizens of contemporary western nations see themselves as obliged in some fashion to the good of their communities.

New forms of media enable citizens to be politically engaged in more diverse fashions. It is certainly the case that with higher levels of overall education, and with the explosion of information technology and social media, there is now more information readily available to more people than ever before. Hegel tells us that, in his own age, legislative assemblies that are open to the public are the greatest educational tools for citizens. For, "it is from this above all that the people can learn the true nature of their interests," and, in such political communities, there is "a much more lively attitude toward the state" than a community in which assemblies take place behind closed doors.[39] People, given the opportunity to see their representatives debate the issues of the day, Hegel argues, are given real insight into the nature of what is at stake and what it is that they themselves truly desire. In essence, legislative debates allow citizens the opportunity to see themselves as they actually are, as rational and multi-faceted beings. They thereby gain a kind of self-consciousness that debate around a dinner table cannot generate.

In the contemporary world, citizens are surrounded by thoughtful and intelligent arguments (as well as those put together with less thought) about the issues of the day. Not only can they watch legislative debates from the comfort of their homes, they can read innumerable analysis of debates and are privy to more alternative perspectives than in any other age. One need only think about the role of both mass and social media in the development of recent citizen revolts in Libya, Egypt, and Syria to see how the new forms of media enable a kind of political engagement that was never before imagined. While even in developed countries the kind of uneducated rabble that Hegel describes in *Elements of the Philosophy of Right* may still exist, the percentage of the population that is educated is surely greater than ever before.[40]

Finally, among people who do not vote, many voice their belief that their single vote is too insignificant or that there is little choice among the candidates and, thus, it does not matter who wins.[41] While such explanations are often frustrating for those who seek to see a more politically engaged citizenry, it may also be an indicator that the *status quo* is actually fine. Hegel argues that the true nature of patriotism is not generally found in great acts of sacrifice for the state, but rather exists more quietly, and that one is perhaps unaware of it within oneself: "in essence it is that disposition which, in normal conditions and circumstances of life, habitually knows that the community is the substantial basis and end."[42] The habit of patriotism, he explains, lies in a general willingness to pay taxes and obedience to the law. "Representational thought, he tells us, "imagines that the state is held together by force; but what holds it together is simply the basic sense of order which everyone possesses."[43] Given the extensive constitutional structures and laws currently in place, that people appear to be apathetic about their government is perhaps a natural and even good thing, as it indicates that people are secure and understand that they will continue to be. It is both a sense that their vote will not change anything, but also, despite seemingly endless complaints, such individuals, when pushed, would presumably also agree that there is not much substantially that has to be changed.

This may not be the same as the ethical self-consciousness that Hegel describes. Yet, Hegel's argument is that the state should incorporate the full interests of its citizens, both particular and universal. Further, he argues that when these interests are not adequately represented, affected individuals will inevitably find the will and necessary voice to seek change. In saying this, Hegel is referring not only to an individual whose particular and idiosyncratic desires are left unattended. Rather, Hegel understands human nature as comprised of both universal and particular elements; we are rational as well as desiring beings, and many of our desires are for rational ends. A political community that does not ultimately reflect the rationality of its citizens will not ultimately be satisfactory. What appears as political apathy might better be described as political satisfaction, or at least sufficient satisfaction that Hegel's world-historical individuals, at least in the relatively stable western world, are not at present needed.

This, however, raises the potential criticism that citizens such as these will not be prepared when an actual crisis does arise. Individuals who have been lulled into a kind of stupor of satisfaction may not be able to shake this habit for the kind of patriotism required when the largest of sacrifices is needed. Hegel, however, argues that it is exactly this kind of general acceptance of the state that ultimately founds the greatest acts of patriotism.[44] Presumably, his argument is that citizens who have grown accustomed to finding their needs and ends within those of their political community will be moved even more fully when the state itself is threatened. Mark Helprin appears to make the same argument in his novel *Freddy and Fredericka*. Prior to describing a particularly inane and, of course, fictional session of the British House of Commons, the book's narrator notes, "without a crisis or a crisis in the making, without a threat to the life of the nation, and in any but a golden age, no leader could be great, and great men seemed out of their element on the green benches of the Commons, having no more place amid the saccharine boo-hoo-hooing and bureaucratic chuckering than Moses in a tea room or Joan of Arc in an aerobic dance class."[45] The corollary of Helprin's scornful observation on the ordinary state of parliamentary institutions is that when a moment of crisis does appear greatness arises from the most unexpected of corners.

The political career of Winston Churchill might supply an example acceptable to Strauss, who admired the English Prime Minister. The shifting sands of Churchill's political fortunes coincided with the general state of peril of his nation. Unquestionably his greatest hour was when England most required his charismatic leadership. Following the war, the tedium of the years of recovery found no place for a Churchill. A more recent example might be seen in the figure of Rudy Giuliani. Immediately prior to the 9/11 attacks, Giuliani seemed to have reached his political "best before date." He had failed in his quest to receive the democratic nod to pursue the Senate seat formerly held by Daniel Patrick Moynihan. Hillary Clinton had the decisive support of the polls. In addition, personal and political scandals were swirling around him and it appeared as if just making it to the end of his term as mayor would be a significant accomplishment. That all changed on 9/11. In the days following, Giuliani's strong leadership was both needed and embraced. This led to a wave of popularity that made him a realistic presidential contender for a time. Yet, upon the resumption of ordinary life in America, Giuliani was restored to his previous stature as just another politician with too much baggage. While no one would suggest Giuliani was another Churchill, both were examples of liberal democracies embracing a noble (even aristocratic, in Churchill's case) vision of leadership in times of crisis. Despite the fact that such leaders were eventually viewed as flawed by their former ardent supporters, the truth of what was sought during the period in which they were needed is evident. The democratic state continues to require certain noble principles—courage, self-sacrifice, and justice—even if these are eclipsed for periods of time by the banality of daily political life. Even more remarkably perhaps, the modern democratic state can supply leadership that rises above the purported desires of the last men when needed. This might suggest that stable regimes, in times of relative peace, have less need of great men and women. Perhaps then some celebration of liberal societies is more appropriate than lamenting the absence of Caesars and Napoleons.

Hegel compares existing political communities to the ugliest of men, letting the reader know that he understood that the Idea of the state would be necessarily transfigured when practically and particularly instantiated. The ethical life he describes in *Elements of the Philosophy of Right* is not envisioned as existing in the manner that he describes. Hegel, however, also tells us that even ugly men can be rational and good. One merely has to look at them in the right light. Contemporary political orders of the western world are examples of Hegel's ugly men. Yet, as we have argued here, this does not preclude rational developments occurring within them. Many conservative critics would argue that the examples we have used are only further evidence of the worsening of the human ethical condition. Hegel, we believe, would disagree. These examples of the acceptance of greater individuality within western political communities serve instead to make citizens stronger and more rational. In the very least, the recognition of the reality of the diverse nature of individual subjectivity, as well as of the power it can have in the lives of individuals and communities, is only prudent and, as Hegel argues, is actually demonstrative of what is objectively true and right. To accept the diversity of individuals serves not to weaken the true or the good, but rather serves as evidence of such elements at work in human life.

NOTES

1. Strauss, "Relativism," in *Relativism and the Study of Man*, 148. Lewis, *The Abolition of Man*, 6.
2. For example, see Drury, *Leo Strauss and the American Right*; Norton, *Leo Strauss and the Politics of American Empire*; and, more recently, Altman, *The German Stranger: Leo Strauss and National Socialism*.
3. Moyar, *Hegel's Conscience*, 207. For an account of the limits of contemporary ethical life in light of Hegel's thought, see Wood, *Hegel's Ethical Thought*, 258–60.
4. Hegel, *Elements of the Philosophy of Right*, sect. 158.
5. Ibid., sect. 163 add.
6. Ibid., sect. 63.
7. Ibid., sect. 164.
8. Ibid., sect. 158.
9. Plato, *The Republic*, 454c.
10. Hegel, *Hegel's Lectures on the Philosophy of Religion*, Vol. 1, 118.
11. Ibid., 119.
12. Ibid., 138.
13. Hegel, *Elements of the Philosophy of Right*, sect. 165.
14. See, MacDonald, *Finding Freedom*; Neuhouser, *Foundations of Hegel's Social Theory*, 274–78.
15. Neuhouser, *Foundations of Hegel's Social Theory*, 277–78.
16. Hegel, *Elements of the Philosophy of Right*, 173A.
17. Neuhouser, *Foundations of Hegel's Social Theory*, 267–68.
18. Hegel, *Elements of the Philosophy of Right*, sect. 183.
19. Ibid., sect. 190.
20. Ibid., sect. 186.
21. Ibid., sect. 187.
22. Augustine, *City of God*, 15, 22, and Augustine, *The Confessions*, 7, 13, 19.
23. Tocqueville, *Democracy in America*, I, 2, 6, 225.
24. Ibid., 183.
25. Zuckert, *The Truth About Leo Strauss* (2006: University of Chicago).
26. Ibid., 57.
27. Fukuyama, *The End of History and the Last Man*, 296.
28. Hegel, *Elements of the Philosophy of Right*, sect. 258.
29. Ibid.
30. Ibid.
31. Ibid.
32. Ibid., sect. 301.
33. Interestingly, since as early as the 1950s academics have been studying the crisis of political apathy among citizens. For example, see Rosenberg, "Some Determinants of Political Apathy," *Public Opinion Quarterly* 18:4 (Winter 1954), 349–66.
34. Hegel, *Elements of the Philosophy of Right*, sect. 311.
35. See Jæger, "What Makes People Support Public Responsibility for Welfare Provision: Self-Interest or Political Ideology? A Longitudinal Approach"; Kaase and Newton, "What People Expect from the State"; and Taylor-Gooby, "Sustaining State Welfare in Hard Times: Who Will Foot the Bill?"
36. Hegel, *Elements of the Philosophy of Right*, sect. 244, note.
37. Ibid., sect. 244, add.
38. On this Hegel, at least in part, agrees. See *Elements of the Philosophy of Right*, sect. 245.
39. Ibid., sect. 315.
40. See also, Best and Krueger, "Analyzing the Representativeness of Internet Political Participation"; Couldry and Markham, "Public Connection through Media Consumption: Between Oversocialization and De-Socialization?"; Stolle, Hooghe, and

Micheletti, "Politics in the Supermarket: Political Consumerism as a Form of Political Participation"; and Vreese, "Digital Renaissance: Young Consumer and Citizen?"

41. For example see, Adams, Dow and Merrill, "The Political Consequences of Alienation-Based and Indifference-Based Voter Abstention: Applications to Presidential Elections"; Merrifield, "The Institutional and Political Factors that Influence Voter Turnout"; and Plane and Gershtenson, "Candidates' Ideological Locations, Abstention, and Turnout in U.S. Midterm Senate Elections."

42. Hegel, *Elements of the Philosophy of Right*, sect. 268.

43. Ibid., sect. 268, add.

44. Ibid., sect. 268.

45. Helprin, *Freddy and Fredericka*, 88.

Conclusion

In the preceding chapters we have sought to both describe Leo Strauss's critique of Hegel's thought and to respond to that critique where appropriate. In doing so, we have argued that not all of what Strauss critiques—historicism, relativism, and nihilism—can be blamed on Hegel. In fact, many of Strauss's concerns about modernity are shared by Hegel. Thus, our argument has two aspects. First, we offer a different interpretation of certain central aspects of Hegel's thought as presented by Strauss. In this regard, we argue, in common with many other scholars, that Strauss's Hegel is really Kojève's reinterpretation of Hegel, at several key moments. Second, we argue that some of the elements of Hegel's thought that Strauss identifies and criticizes can be defended. In doing this, we are defending elements of modern society against Strauss's criticism, and suggesting that the roots of this defense can be found in Hegel's religious and political philosophy.

Thus, in chapter three, we advanced the position that Strauss's avoidance of any serious engagement with Christian philosophy or theology leaves him at a distinct disadvantage when interpreting Hegel. While we do not engage in a detailed exploration of Hegel's relation to orthodox Christian doctrine, we suggest that the key doctrinal elements of that tradition—the incarnation, atonement, resurrection and the trinity, not to mention Christian anthropology—are all present in Hegel's thought and contribute fundamentally to the form and content of his argument. Doull expresses the relationship this way:

> The Phenomenology of Spirit, as an introduction to the science of Logic and the other parts of the Hegelian system, does not lead everyone to the system, whatever presuppositions one may hold as to how, if at all, 'spirit' can be known philosophically. What 'spirit' means is taken to be known through the Christian religion: the triune God in himself, the creation of irrational nature and of the rational creature, implicitly spiritual, the division or 'fall' of the rational creature, the revelation of what God is in the incarnation, death and resurrection of the Son, the conversion thereby of the division into a moment of concrete spiritual form unifying God and the human individual. That this belief—expressed in a thinking which used natural relations for that which was beyond them—could be known as true also for thought had long since been the interest of philosophical Christians; a necessary interest since, for other than philosophical thought, the *Vorstellung* was incredible.[1]

The question of Hegel's own orthodoxy is surely less easily settled now in a period where the manifold variants of protestant religious expression are nearly matched by the variety of theologies and pieties found even within Catholicism. Nevertheless, the central Christian doctrine of the reconciliation of the universal and particular in a person who is at once human and divine is the theological foundation for the account of modernity that Hegel presents. It is this reconciliation—the union of objectivity and subjectivity—in political form that Hegel views as a positive development (indeed, an absolute development) while Strauss views the same as either impossible or ruinous to human good.

Certainly, the New Testament reflects this union of the divine principle with human subjectivity. While the Incarnation is the concrete embodiment of this truth in history, the Gospels record numerous instances of Jesus challenging abstract law and asserting the need for an inward recognition of the principle. This distinction between the letter and the spirit imposes an internal moral responsibility on believers. No one is exempt from this project of self-governance. This is ultimately a democratizing moral imperative. All must take responsibility for their own ethical lives. This requires a respect for individuals as moral agents that in turn produces a radical equality.

The consequences of this "freedom from the law" are wide-ranging and consume much of moral and political philosophy in succeeding centuries.[2] For example, Augustine engages in a protracted debate with the Pelagians over the proper relation of external works to the internal principle of faith. This, in turn, continues to be a central tension for another twelve centuries and beyond, finding its most explicit discussion in the protestant reformers. The insistence by the reformers, in general, on the inward subjective response of the individual believer to the objective gospel proclamation, is the hallmark of both reformed theology and those polities influenced by it. Lutheran Germany, as well as Protestant England, and eventually America, find increasing space for individual subjectivity in religious (and other social) expression. This is not an immediate process; the laws enforcing Protestant conformity are as rigid and brutal as their Catholic counterparts for generations in Europe. However, out of this religious revolution emerges a consensus in Europe and generally in the New World, that the Christian religion requires freedom for the individual and cannot be imposed by the state. This, in turn, opens the door for religious pluralism and requires religious tolerance. Most liberal democracies eventually recognize this and reflect it in various forms of constitutional guarantees of freedom of religious thought and expression.

For Strauss, the key distinction between Athens and Jerusalem, as we have argued, can only be maintained by avoiding consideration of the development of Christian thought. The origin of this distinction lies with the early church author, Tertullian, who wrote:

> What indeed has Athens to do with Jerusalem? What has the Academy to do with the Church? What have heretics to do with Christians? Our instruction comes from the porch of Solomon, who had himself taught that the Lord should be sought in simplicity of heart. Away with all attempts to produce a Stoic, Platonic, and dialectic Christianity! We want no curious disputation after possessing Christ Jesus, no inquisition after receiving the gospel! When we believe, we desire no further belief. For this is our first article of faith, that there is nothing which we ought to believe besides.[3]

It is important to remember that Tertullian was condemned by the church as a heretic (although not, it must be confessed, on this point). His refusal to take up ancient philosophy is not shared by the entirety of the Christian intellectual tradition that follows, even if the proper relation between faith and reason will continue to be the struggle of Christian thinkers. However, the question raised by Tertullian is never seriously considered by Strauss in the light of the claims of Christian theology or philosophy. Hegel, on the other hand, seeks to resolve exactly this issue—the relation between Athens and Jerusalem—and his *Lectures on the Philosophy of Religion* point to Christianity as the perfect reconciliation of the principles represented by those two cities.

Of course, since the collapse of Aquinas's medieval synthesis, the ground was laid for the separation of faith and reason that Aquinas had painstakingly united in the *Summa Theologica*. Ockham, Cusa, and Marsilius of Padua, in the generations immediately following Aquinas, argued variously for a separation of secular and spiritual thought and institutions. By leaping over the first thirteen centuries of Christian thought and beginning with Marsilius, then moving quickly to Machiavelli and Hobbes, Strauss avoids any argument that might reconcile, or at least not dichotomize, faith and reason, theology and philosophy. The Protestant thinkers (of whom Machiavelli was perhaps a kind of strange forerunner and Hobbes was a product) require a new formulation of this relationship. The collapse of medieval political institutions was intimately connected with this reconsideration of the place of religious authority to human reason and freedom.

In Kant, the separation of belief from reason found its clearest and strongest modern advocate. The powerful arguments of the *Critique of Pure Reason* demonstrate the inadequacy of the medieval synthesis to the modern scientific mind. In large measure, Hegel's philosophy of religion, and his metaphysics and ontology, are a response to Kant. Strauss is sympathetic to Kant's separation of belief and reason and we have argued that this is near the root of Strauss's sympathy for the anti-Hegelian positions that arise in the nineteenth century (e.g., Nietzsche) and move through his own teachers (e.g., Heidegger) into the twentieth. As much as Strauss dissents from Nietzsche and Heidegger, at many points his fundamental sympathy for Kantian metaphysics against Hegel's places him in crucial agreement with the very existentialist thinkers that he blames for many of modernity's ills.

Against Strauss we have argued that Hegel is not an atheist, advocating a merely secular horizon for human beings. Instead, Hegel's emphasis on subjectivity and human freedom is posited in relation to, and in tension with, the Absolute. There are, in fact, eternal objective principles insisted upon by Hegel. However, these principles are necessarily mediated through human subjectivity. The peculiar form of the Christian religion sets forth and requires a taking up of free subjectivity into the Absolute. Put another way, the Absolute is made known in human subjectivity. Obviously, this admits readily of all the forms of interpretation from atheism, through pantheism, that readers of Hegel have variously claimed since his death. Instead, we have argued that Hegel's religious thought is compatible with much of Christian theology and, in fact, that Christianity leads to the institutional forms advocated by Hegel. Notwithstanding this, it is ironic, although perhaps not surprising, that the Christian church has not always realized the content of its thought, and, instead, often simply aligns itself with the state in its various forms or with the personality of its leader.

The consideration of Hegel's religious thought and our identification of the failure of Strauss to take seriously Hegel's Christianity provides a foundation for our interpretation of Strauss's treatment of Hegel's political thought. We have argued that Hegel's apprehension of the consequences of Christian doctrine, with respect to the role of subjectivity and freedom, is foundational for his political thought. It is our position that just as Strauss either ignores or misunderstands Hegel's religious positions, so consequently he misunderstands and thereby levels incorrect criticisms towards Hegel's political philosophy. This is partially because of the intervention of Kojève, through whose lens Strauss reads Hegel.

On this we agree with Strauss: the guiding principle of modernity is freedom. We further agree that Hegel is the great champion of this position. We disagree about the origins of this principle, finding it in the very heart of Christianity, rather than in the various waves of modernity set against antiquity. We further disagree about the value of this modern principle and about Strauss's claim that it is irreconcilable with either virtue or the human good in general.

Another major element of Strauss's criticism of Hegel concerns the idea of progress toward a world homogenous state. We have argued, along with others, that this element of Strauss's argument is based upon Kojève's reading of Hegel. Kojève's reduction of the moving force of progress in Hegel's thought to the passions and the struggle for recognition distorts Hegel's meaning materially. While the *Phenomenology* portrays this struggle, it is only one moment in the dialectic of human development towards self-consciousness. The *Philosophy of Right*, and the *Philosophy of History*, fill in this picture considerably. Human passions are only part of the nature that we use to appropriate the Absolute. Ultimately, the Idea, recognized by our rational faculty, directs human progress towards the manifestation of the truth in the world.

The driving force behind progress toward the ethical state is the desire for freedom. This is a rational end in itself. However, it also accords with our greatest desire. The role of modern institutions is to reconcile our desire for recognition, freedom, and a host of lesser goods, to our rational end. That such a task will be imperfectly executed is necessarily the case because of the variety and contingency of human existence in the world. In the same way, this variety precludes a single form of the manifestation of the principle of freedom. In "[recognizing] in the semblance of the temporal and transient the substance which is immanent and the eternal which is present,"[4] we are acknowledging that the appearance of the eternal good need not be homogenous in form. In fact, Hegel foresees individual states as necessarily continuing to represent the "ethical whole" amid diverse "passions, interests and ends."[5]

In the end, Hegel's argument does not lead simply to an abstract mutual recognition of our subjective existence. Nor does it envision the collapse of subjectivity into an objective oneness. We are Spirit insofar as we unite subjectivity with the objective good. The progress of history, as understood by Hegel, is towards a state that at once allows us to realize our subjective freedom while also directing us towards, and grounding us in, the objective good.

For Hegel, three spheres are essential in the development of ethical political individuals—the family, civil society, and the state. Strauss would presumably find the forms of each of these three elements to be defective in the modern world. The swapping of freedom in place of virtue is alleged to be at the root of human corruption. From an ancient perspective, this position makes perfect sense. The change that Christianity makes to the ancient account of anthropology and the relationship between the particular and the universal brings forth the possibility of an alternate account. Our *telos* is both knowable and attainable. Only by knowing ourselves as free can we enter into this new kingdom. Yet, this freedom is not solely constituted by our subjectivity. Our free wills are united to the eternal *logos* present within us. The family, civil society, and the state must all reflect both sides of this union. We learn to will the objective good by habituation in willing the good for others. This is a principle of modern family life, wherein families are less certainly held together by natural bonds and increasingly are seen to require free and rational wills to function properly. Similarly, civil society is an arena that allows us to pursue our subjective desires, yet we are taught that they can only be satisfied by acknowledging principles beyond ourselves. These principles are instantiated in the law, but are also represented to us in the need to accord respect and dignity to others in daily life. New laws, reflecting newly recognized rights, are imposed initially (and perhaps abstractly), but insofar as they are consistent with the principles of this modern society then they will eventually come to be freely acknowledged and observed. Everything from equal rights for women, thought once to be counter to natural law, to the recognition of the validity of different sexual orientations are representative of the capacity of civil society to adapt as it more completely expresses its own principles.

Recently, among others, the American philosopher and writer Kwame Anthony Appiah has argued for a perspective consistent with liberalism that he identifies as "cosmopolitanism."[6] This involves the extension of the mutual respect that members of one society have for one another to all people. Rather than necessarily pointing towards a single world government, or world homogenous state, this position recognizes the universal truth of liberalism. The particular contingent circumstances of individual cultures need not be threatened by such a cosmopolitan outlook. However, the long intellectual and moral struggle that individual liberal regimes have experienced in actualizing their principles can be expected to be the experience of those engaged in the extension of the same principles to a wider community of people elsewhere.

It is not immediately clear, for example, if liberal democracies are obliged to intervene in the affairs of societies that are perceived to operate with less than liberal principles. That such a debate should be part of the social discourse of liberal societies does not deny the western consensus around the value of liberty. Even those who are non-interventionists, or at least those who oppose military intervention, often seek other means of promoting liberal social transformation. Both left and right often condemn human rights abuses in other societies, while differing vastly on how to respond to those abuses. The nearly worldwide abhorrence of apartheid in South Africa, the mobilization of both conservative and leftist opinion in liberal societies against repressive regimes in the Middle East in 2010 and 2011, and such formal documents as the United Nations Declaration of Human Rights, are all signs of the development of a shared account of the importance of certain preconditions for human flourishing. While it is easy to list those elements of modern society that are not in conformity with the ideal of an ethical state, the real question is whether these are signs of progress towards a more ethical society.

None of the foregoing directly responds to the charge that modernity has produced a race of last men. In the end, Hegel's argument would have to be that the conditions for a virtuous life exist wherever liberty exists. While the splendid achievements of ancient Athens do not seem to have a precise modern parallel, it would be hard to demonstrate that there are fewer people than ever pursuing philosophy or attempting to live the good life. Indeed, if one were to accept the Christian account that the good life involves charity as much as wisdom, one might be able to argue that most liberal regimes are considerably less harsh and more charitable than their ancient predecessors. Social welfare systems, while under economic strain at present, still reflect a societal commitment to care for the disadvantaged at a cost to everyone else. Moreover, in liberal societies, individuals are free to pursue the life of the mind and whatever spiritual path they choose. These opportunities are available, for the first time in history, to women as well as men. Higher education is accessible for more people in our time than at any time throughout history. A man of mixed race, born to no title and without wealth, can receive a first-class education and become president of the United States. To dismiss the elements of good in these indicators requires perhaps a different account of good than the Christian definition offers.

For Hegel, modernity is about the reconciliation of individual subjectivity with objective truth. The institutions of modern liberal democracies are ethical in form insofar as they are constructed to achieve just this goal. The rule of law is predicated not only upon a certain liberal account of rights, but also upon the belief that there are objective goods, which positive laws seek to reflect. The refusal to delineate the particular objective goods protected by liberal constitutions does not mean that the societies founded upon these institutions do not believe in such goods. Rather, in the ethical state, as understood by Hegel, the individual subject is obliged to appropriate those goods within the context of his contingent circumstances. The state seeks to guarantee freedom for this activity. This is the only way that individuals may find a free subjective relation to the Absolute good. Of course this allows many (and messy) paths to the realization of such an end. We might recall Robert Pippin's insight that "All the Hegelian needs to show is that, as rational individuals (even if not wholly rational), there will be no rational basis for any dissatisfaction [within the modern world]."[7] Our liberty dictates that we can pursue either those ends that lead to satisfaction or those ends that are self-destructive.

The objections that Leo Strauss raises against modern society are easily sustained in many respects. A liberal and egalitarian society is less interested in singular examples of greatness and even distrusts conspicuous nobility. *Techne* is more valued than *sophia*. The vulgarity and irrationality of much popular entertainment is a frequently cited and easy target by writers less profound and subtle than Strauss. Certainly, if we contrast *Jersey Shore* to the plays of Sophocles, condemnation of the culture that produced the former and is ignorant of the latter is simple. The last men have clearly won, if we rest with this type of comparison. However, the argument of this book is that in a world wherein Spirit is made manifest in the lives of contingent and free beings, more people than ever before have opportunities to pursue the good life for human beings. The sheer multitude of choices possible for people in terms of the exercise of their wills in countless spheres inevitably produces results that are disappointing to those who choose differently.

But, our argument is not simply that it is possible to pursue the good life in modernity. That would be the faintest of praises and one that even Strauss would concede in modernity's favor. Rather, our argument, echoing Hegel's, is that despite the deprivations that arise from human selfishness and rejection of reason, the Absolute not only endures in the world, but is increasingly manifest. Perhaps it is possible to see the nihilistic elements of modern technological culture as defective forms of western rationality and freedom, rather than as illustrations of the inherent and inevitably destructive consequences of those principles.[8] While the left and the right respectively see western reason on the one hand, or subjectivity and freedom on the other, as the source of our contemporary decadence, Hegel asserts that both must be aspects of our lives as spirit.

In their proper forms, duly accommodating the truth of the other, reason and subjectivity do not produce last men. Human beings who know themselves to be free, at home in the world of particularity and contingency, are able (in this freedom) to see the Absolute present both in the world and as an object of thought, and are the true children of modernity. The persistence of theism in our post-modern world (and not only in radicalized, anti-liberal forms) suggests a yearning for something beyond the satisfaction of mere sensual appetites. For Hegel, this is not merely a vestige of pre-liberal ignorance, but rather an enduring aspect of human beings' nature as Spirit. The recognition of the true nature of the family, as grounded in willing the good to others with whom a true bond of love is formed, the extension of liberal civil institutions to include those previously marginalized or excluded, and the grounding of states that recognize both human freedom and the objective good are all means by which the modern world is moving, however haltingly, towards a more complete realization of an ethical society.

NOTES

1. James Doull, "Hegel's Phenomenology and Post-Modern Thought," *Animus* 5 (2000).
2. Galatians, 5.
3. Tertullian, *The Prescription Against Heretics*, chapter VII.
4. Hegel, *Elements of the Philosophy of Right*, sect. 20.
5. Ibid., sect. 340.
6. Kwame Anthome Appiah, *Cosmopolitanism: Ethics in a World of Strangers.* (New York: W.W. Norton, 2006).
7. Robert B. Pippin, "Being, Time, and Politics: The Strauss-Kojève Debate," 157.
8. Doull, p. 349.

Bibliography

Adams, James, Jay Dow, and Samuel Merrill III. "The Political Consequences of Alienation-Based and Indifference-Based Voter Abstention: Applications to Presidential Elections." *Political Behavior* 28:1 (Mar., 2006): 65–86.

Allen, Michael P. "Hegel Between Non-Domination and Expressive Freedom: Capabilities, Perspectives and Democracy." *Philosophy and Social Criticism* 32:4 (June, 2006): 493–512.

Altman, William H. F. "Leo Strauss on 'German Nihilism': Learning the Art of Writing." *Journal of the History of Ideas* 68:4 (October, 2007): 587–612.

———. *The German Stranger: Leo Strauss and National Socialism.* Maryland: Lexington Books, 2010.

Anderson, Sybol Cook. *Hegel's Theory of Recognition: From Oppression to Ethical Modernity.* New York: Continuum, 2009.

Aquinas, *Summa Theologia,* vol.1. Edited by Thomas Gilby. London: Eryre & Spottiswoode, 1964.

Aristotle. *Metaphysics.* Translated by Hugh Tredennick. Cambridge: Harvard University Press, 1933.

———. *Nicomachean Ethics.* Translated by Terence Irwin. Indianapolis: Hackett Publishing Co., 2000.

———. *Politics.* Translated by C.D.C. Reeve. Indianapolis: Hackett Publishing Co., 1998.

Augustine. *The City of God against the Pagans.* Edited by R. W. Dyson. Cambridge: Cambridge University Press, 1998.

———. *Confessions.* Translated by Chadwick. Oxford: Oxford University Press, 1991.

Bernstein, Richard J. "Why Hegel Now?" *The Review of Metaphysics* 31:1 (September, 1977): 29–60.

Best, Samuel J. and Brian S. Krueger. "Analyzing the Representativeness of Internet Political Participation." *Political Behavior* 27:2 (Jun., 2005): 183–216.

Bloom Allan. *The Closing of the American Mind.* New York: Schuster and Schuster, 1987.

Cooper, Barry. *The End of History: An Essay on Modern Hegelianism.* Toronto: University of Toronto Press, 1984.

Couldry, Nick and Tim Markham. "Public Connection through Media Consumption: Between Oversocialization and De-Socialization?" *Annals of the American Academy of Political and Social Science* 608 (Nov., 2006): 251–69.

Dallmayr, Fred R. *G.W.F. Hegel: Modernity and Politics.* London: Sage Publications, Inc., 1993.

Dante, *The Divine Comedy: Purgatory.* Vol. 2. Translated by Dorothy L. Sayers. New York: Penguin Classics, 1955.

Doull, James A. "Hegel on the English Reform Bill." *Animus* 5 (2000): 43–54, http://www2.swgc.mun.ca/animus/Articles/Volume%205/doull5b.pdf.

———. *Philosophy and Freedom: The Legacy of James Doull.* Edited by David G. Peddle and Neil G. Robertson. Toronto: University of Toronto Press, 2003.

Drury, Shadia B. *Leo Strauss and the American Right.* Palgrave Macmillan: London, 1999.

———. "Saving America." Evatt Foundation (11 September 2003).

Dubose, Todd. "Bondage, and the Formation of 'Homo Religiosus.'" *Journal of Religion and Health* 39:3 (Fall 2000): 217–26.

Fackenheim, Emil. *The Religious Dimension in Hegel's Thought.* Boston: Beacon Press, 1970.

Franco, Paul. "Hegel and Liberalism." *The Review of Politics* 59:4 (Autumn, 1997): 831–60.

———. *Hegel's Philosophy of Freedom*. New Haven: Yale University Press, 1999.

Fukuyama, Francis. *The End of History and the Last Man*. New York: Harper Perennial, 1993.

Harris, Errol E. *The Spirit of Hegel*. New Jersey: Humanities Press, 1993.

Hodgson, Peter C. *Hegel and Christian Theology: A Reading of the Lectures on the Philosophy of Religion*. Oxford: Oxford University Press, 2005.

Garza, Abel Jr. "Hegel's Critique of Liberalism and Natural Law: Reconstructing Ethical Life." *Law and Philosophy* 9:4 (1990–1991): 371–98.

Gourevitch, Victor. "Philosophy and Politics," I-II. *The Review of Metaphysics*. 22 (1968): 58–84; 281–328.

Grier, Philip T. "The End of History, and the Return of History." *The Owl of Minerva* 21:2 (Spring 1990): 131–44.

Gunnell, John G. "Strauss before Straussianism: Reason, Revelation, and Nature." *The Review of Politics* 53:1 (Winter, 1991): 53–74.

Hegel, G.W.F. *Aesthetics: Lectures on Fine Arts*. Translated by T. M. Knox. 2 vols. Oxford: Clarendon Press, 1975.

———. *Elements of the Philosophy of Right*. Translated by H. B. Nisbet. Cambridge: Cambridge University Press, 1991.

———. *The Encyclopedia Logic*. Translated by T. F. Geraets, W. A. Suchting, and H. S. Harris. Cambridge: Hackett Publishing Company, Inc., 1991.

———. *Lectures on The Philosophy of Religion*. Translated by R. F. Brown, P. C. Hodgson, and J. M. Stewart with the assistance of H. S. Harris. 3 vols. Berkeley: University of California Press, 1987.

———. *Phenomenology of Spirit*. Translated by A. V. Miller. Oxford: Oxford University Press, 1977.

———. *The Philosophy of History*. Translated by J. Sibree. New York: Dover Publications, Inc., 1956.

———. *Philosophy of Mind*. Translated by A. V. Miller. Oxford: Clarendon Press, 1971.

———. *System of Ethical Life and First Philosophy of Spirit*. Translated by H.S. Harris and T. M. Knox. Albany: State University of New York Press, 1979.

Helprin, Mark. *Freddy and Fredericka*. New York: Penguin Press, 2005.

Houlgate, Stephen. *Freedom, Truth and History: An Introduction to Hegel's Philosophy*. New York: Routledge, 1991.

Jæger, Mads Meier. "What Makes People Support Public Responsibility for Welfare Provision: Self-Interest or Political Ideology? A Longitudinal Approach." *Acta Sociologica* 49:3 (Sep., 2006): 321–38.

Jaeschke, Walter. *Reason in Religion: The Foundations of Hegel's Philosophy of Religion*. Berkeley: University of California Press, 1990.

Jansses, David. *Between Athens and Jerusalem: Philosophy, Prophecy, and Politics in Leo Strauss's Early Thought*. Albany: State University of New York Press, 2008.

Jung, Hwa Yol. "Leo Strauss's Conception of Political Philosophy: A Critique." *The Review of Politics* 29:4 (October, 1967): 492–517.

Kaase, Max and Kenneth Newton. "What People Expect from the State: Plus ca Change." *British and European Social Attitudes. How Britain Differs: The 15th Report*. Edited by Roger Jowell et al. Aldershot: Ashgate, 1998.

Kainz, Howard P. *G. W. F. Hegel*. Ohio: Ohio University Press, 1996.

Kaufman, Alexander. "Hegel and the Ontological Critique of Liberalism." *The American Political Science Review* 91: 4 (December 1997): 807–17.

Kaufmann, Walter, ed. *Debating the Political Philosophy of Hegel*. New Brunswick: Aldine Transaction, 2010.

———. *Hegel*. New York: Doubleday, 1965.

Kelly, George Armstrong, "Hegel and 'The Present Standpoint.'" *Political Theory* 4:1 (February 1976): 45–63.

———. "Politics and Philosophy in Hegel," *Polity* 9:1 (Autumn 1976): 3–18.

———. *Hegel's Retreat from Eleusis*. Princeton: Princeton University Press, 1978.

———. "Politics and Philosophy in Hegel." *Polity* 9:1 (Autumn, 1976): 3–18.

Kennington, Richard. "Strauss's Natural Right and History." *The Review of Metaphysics* 35:1 (September, 1981): 57–86.

Kojève, Alexandre. *Introduction to the Reading of Hegel: Lectures on the* Phenomenology of Spirit. Edited by Allan Bloom. New York: Cornell University Press, 1969.

Lakeland, Paul. *The Politics of Salvation: The Hegelian Idea of the State*. Albany: State University of New York Press, 1984.

Lewis, C. S. *The Abolition of Man*. New York: HarperOne, 2001.

Lewis, Thomas A. *Freedom and Tradition in Hegel: Reconsidering Anthropology, Ethics and Religion*. Notre Dame: University of Notre Dame Press, 2005.

Lilla, Mark "Reading Strauss in Beijing: China's Strange Taste in Western Philosophers." *New Republic* (December 30, 2010): 14–17.

Locke, John. *Two Treatises of Government*. Cambridge: Cambridge University Press, 1988.

MacDonald, Sara. *Finding Freedom: Hegel's Philosophy and the Emancipation of Women*. Montreal: McGill Queen's University Press, 2008.

Machiavelli. *The Prince*. Translated by Harvey C. Mansfield, Jr. Chicago: University of Chicago Press, 1985.

Mattarrese, Craig. "Hegel on Freedom." *Philosophy Compass* 2:2 (March, 2007): 170–86.

McDaniel, Robb A. "The Nature of Inequality: Uncovering the Modern in Leo Strauss's Idealist Ethics." *Political Theory* 26:3 (June, 1998): 317–45.

Meier, Heinrich. *Leo Strauss and the Theologico-Political Problem*. Translated by Marcus Bertrand. Cambridge: Cambridge University Press, 2006.

Merrifield, John. "The Institutional and Political Factors that Influence Voter Turnout" *Public Choice* 77:3 (Nov., 1993): 657–67.

Merrill, Clark A. "Leo Strauss's Indictment of Christian Philosophy." *The Review of Politics* 62:1 (Winter, 2000): 77–105.

Minowitz, Peter. *Straussophobia: Defending Leo Strauss and Straussians against Shadia Drury and Other Accusers*. Lanham: Lexington Books, 2009.

Moggach, Douglas, ed. *Politics, Religion, and Art*. Illinois: Northwestern University Press, 2011.

Morgan, Michael L. "The Curse of Historicity: The Rose of History in Leo Strauss's Jewish Thought." *The Journal of Religion* 61:4 (October, 1981): 345–63.

Moyar, Dean. *Hegel's Conscience*. Oxford: Oxford University Press, 2010.

Neuhouser, Frederick. *Foundations of Hegel's Social Theory*. Cambridge: Harvard University Press, 2000.

Nietzsche, Friedrich. *On the Advantage and Disadvantage of History for Life*. Translated by Peter Preuss. Indianapolis: Hackett Publishing Company, 1980.

———. *The Genealogy of Morals*. Translated by Walter Kaufmann. New York: Vintage Books, 1989.

Norton, Ann. *Leo Strauss and the Politics of American Empire*. New Haven: Yale University Press, 2004.

Orr, Susan. *Jerusalem and Athens: Reason and Revelation in the Work of Leo Strauss*. Boston: Rowman & Littlefield Publishers, Inc., 1995.

Pangle, Thomas. *Leo Strauss: An Introduction to His Thought and Intellectual Legacy*. Baltimore: John Hopkins University Press, 2006.

Patten, Alan. *Hegel's Idea of Freedom*. New York: Oxford University Press, 1999.

Pelczynski, Z. A., ed. *Hegel's Political Philosophy*. Cambridge: Cambridge University Press, 1971.

———. ed. *The State and Civil Society: Studies in Hegel's Political Philosophy*. Cambridge: Cambridge University Press, 1984.

Plane, Dennis L. and Joseph Gershtenson. "Candidates' Ideological Locations, Abstention, and Turnout in U.S. Midterm Senate Elections." *Political Behavior* 26:1 (Mar., 2004): 69–93.

Plato. *Euthydemus*. Translated by Rosamond Kent Sprague. Indianapolis: Hackett Publishing, Inc., 1993.
———. *Gorgias*. Translated by Donald J. Zeyl. Indianapolis: Hackett Publishing, Inc., 1987.
———. *Plato on Love*. Edited by C. D. C. Reeve. Indianapolis: Hackett Publishing, Co., 2006.
———. *Republic*. Translated by G. M. A. Grube. Indianapolis: Hackett Publishing Co., 1992.
Pippin, Robert B. "Being, Time, and Politics: The Strauss-Kojève Debate." *History and Theory* 32:2 (May, 1993): 138–61.
———. "Hegel on Political Philosophy and Political Actuality," *Inquiry* 53:5 (October 2010): 401–16.
———. *Hegel on Self-Consciousness: Desire and Death in the* Phenomenology of Spirit. Princeton: Princeton University Press, 2011.
———. *Modernism as a Philosophical Problem*. Oxford: Blackwell Publishers, 1999.
———. "The Modern World of Leo Strauss." *Political Theory* 20:3 (August, 1992): 448–72.
———. *The Persistence of Subjectivity: On the Kantian Aftermath*. Cambridge: Cambridge University Press, 2005.
Reardon, Bernard M. G. *Hegel's Philosophy of Religion*. London: MacMillian Press, 1977.
Robertson, Neil. "Leo Strauss's Platonism." *Animus* 4 (1994), http://www.mun.ca/animus/1999vol4/roberts4.htm.
Rosen, Stanley. *G. W. F Hegel*. New York: Yale University Press, 1974.
Rosenberg, Morris. "Some Determinants of Political Apathy." *The Public Opinion Quarterly* 18:4 (Winter, 1954–1955): 349–66
Roth, Michael S. "A Problem of Recognition: Alexander Kojève and the End of History." *History and Theory* 24: 3 (October, 1985): 293–306.
———. "A Note of Kojève's Phenomenology of Right." *Political Theory* 11:3 (August, 1983): 447–50.
Schall, James V. "A Latitude for Statesmanship? Strauss on Thomas." *The Review of Politics* 53:1 (Winter, 1991): 126–45.
Shklar, Judith N. *Freedom and Independence: A Study of the Political Ideas of Hegel's "Phenomenology of Mind."* Cambridge: Cambridge University Press, 1976.
Shorris, Earl. "Ignoble Liars: Leo Strauss, George Bush, and the Philosophy of Mass Deception." *Harper's Magazine* 308:1849 (June 2004): 65–71.
Sinnerbrink, Robert. *Understanding Hegelianism*. Stocksfield: Acumen, 2007.
Smith, Steven B., ed. *The Cambridge Companion to Leo Strauss*. Cambridge: Cambridge University Press, 2009.
———. "Leo Strauss: Between Athens and Jerusalem." *The Review of Politics* 53:1 (Winter, 1991), 75–99.
———. "Hegel's Critique of Liberalism," *The American Political Science Review*. 80:1 (March, 1986): 121–39.
———. *Hegel's Critique of Liberalism*. Chicago: University of Chicago Press, 1989.
———. "What is 'Right' in Hegel's Philosophy of Right." *The American Political Science Review* 83:1 (March, 1989): 3–18.
Soll, Ivan. *An Introduction to Hegel's Metaphysics*. Chicago: University of Chicago Press, 1969.
Sorensen, Kim. "Revelation and Reason in Leo Strauss." *The Review of Politics* 65:3 (Summer, 2003): 383–408.
Speight, Allen. *The Philosophy of Hegel*. Montreal: McGill-Queen's University Press, 2008.
Steinkraus, Warren E. *New Studies in Hegel's Philosophy*. New York: Holt, Rinehart and Winston, 1971.
Stolle, Dietlind, Marc Hooghe, and Michele Micheletti. "Politics in the Supermarket: Political Consumerism as a Form of Political Participation." *International Political Science Review / Revue internationale de science politique* 26: 3 (Jul., 2005): 245–69.

Strauss, Leo. *An Introduction to Political Philosophy*. Edited by Hilael Gilden. Detroit: Wayne State University Press, 1989.

———. *The City and Man*. Chicago: Rand McNally, 1964.

———. "The Crisis of our Time." In *The Predicament of Modern Politics*, edited by Harold J. Spaeth. Detroit: University of Detroit Press, 1964.

———. *Faith and Political Philosophy: The Correspondence Between Leo Strauss and Eric Voegelin, 1934–1964*. Edited by Peter Emberley and Barry Cooper. Pennsylvania: The Pennsylvania State University Press, 1993.

———. *Jewish Philosophy and the Crisis of Modernity*. Edited by Kenneth Hart Green. Albany: State University of New York, 1997.

———. "Lectures on the *Philosophy of History*," Leo Strauss Papers [Box 9, Folder 4, Lecture, 12], Special Collections Research Center, University of Chicago Library.

———. "The Liberalism of Classical Political Philosophy." *The Review of Metaphysics* 12:3 (March, 1959): 390–493.

———. "Marsilius of Padua." In *History of Political Philosophy*. Edited by Leo Strauss and Joseph Cropsey. Chicago: University of Chicago Press, 1987.

———. *Natural Right and History*. Chicago: University of Chicago Press, 1953.

———. "On the Interpretation of Genesis." *L'Homme*. 21:1 (janvier–mars 1981): 5–20.

———. *On Tyranny*. New York: Free Press, 1991.

———. *Persecution and the Art of Writing*. Chicago: University of Chicago Press, 1964.

———. *The Political Philosophy of Thomas Hobbes*. Chicago: University of Chicago Press, 1996.

———. *Political Philosophy: Six Essays by Leo Strauss*. Edited by Hilael Gildin. Indianapolis: University of Chicago Press, 1975.

———. "Progress or Return," *Modern Judaism* 1:1 (May, 1981), 17–45.

———. "Reason and Revelation." In *Leo Strauss and the Theologico-Political Problem*. Edited by Heinrich Meier. Cambridge: Cambridge University Press, 2006.

———. *The Rebirth of Classical Political Rationalism*. Indianapolis: University of Chicago Press, 1989.

———. "Relativism." In *Relativism and the Study of Man*. Edited by Helmut Schoeck and James W. Wiggins. Princeton: D. Van Nostrand, 1961, 135–57.

———. *Studies in Platonic Philosophy*. Chicago: University of Chicago Press, 1985.

———. *What Is Political Philosophy? and Other Studies*. Glencoe: The Free Press, 1959.

Tanquay, Daniel. *Leo Strauss: An Intellectual Biography*. New Haven: Yale University Press, 2003.

Tarcov, Nathan. "Philosophy and History: Tradition and Interpretation in the Work of Leo Strauss." *Polity* 16:1 (Autumn, 1993): 5–29.

Taylor, Charles. *Hegel*. Cambridge: Cambridge University Press, 1975.

———. *Hegel and Modern Society*. Cambridge: Cambridge University Press, 1979.

Taylor-Gooby, Peter. "Sustaining State Welfare in Hard Times: Who Will Foot the Bill?" *Journal of European Social Policy* 11: 2 (May, 2001): 133–47.

Thucydides. *The Peloponnesian War*. Translated by Steven Lattimore. Indianapolis: Hackett Publishing Company, Inc., 1998.

Tocqueville, Alexis de. *Democracy in America*. Translated by Harvey Mansfield. Chicago: University of Chicago Press, 2000.

Tertullian. *The Prescription Against Heretics*. Translated by the Rev. Peter Holmes. Chapter VII. www.Tertullian.org.

Vreese, Claes H. de. "Digital Renaissance: Young Consumer and Citizen?," *Annals of the American Academy of Political and Social Science* 611 (May, 2007): 207–16.

Westphal, Merold. *Hegel, Freedom, and Modernity*. New York: State University of New York Press, 1992.

Williams, Robert R. *Hegel's Ethics of Recognition*. Berkeley: University of California Press, 1997.

Williamson, Raymond Keith. *Introduction to Hegel's Philosophy of Religion*. New York: State University of New York, 1984.

Wood, Allen W. *Hegel's Ethical Thought*. Cambridge: Cambridge University Press, 1990.

Zuckert, Catherine and Michael Zuckert. *The Truth about Leo Strauss: Political Philosophy and American Democracy*. Chicago: University of Chicago Press, 2006.

———. *Postmodern Platos: Nietzsche, Heidegger, Gadamer, Strauss, and Derrida*. Chicago: Chicago University Press, 1996.

Index

About the Authors

Sara MacDonald is an associate professor and the director of the Great Books Programme at St. Thomas University, a liberal arts college in Fredericton NB, Canada. She obtained her B.A. from St. Thomas University and her M.A. and Ph.D. from Fordham University. She is the author *of Finding Freedom: Hegel's Philosophy and the Emancipation of Women* (McGill-Queen's, 2008). Her next book for Lexington Press, also coauthored with Barry Craig, is a study of the novels of Mark Helprin.

Barry Craig is an associate professor in the Department of Philosophy and Vice-President (Academic) at St. Thomas University, a liberal arts college in Fredericton NB, Canada. He obtained his B.A. from the University of King's College in Halifax NS, his M.A. from Dalhousie University, and his Ph.D. from the University of Wales. He is the author of *Apostle to the Wilderness* (Fairleigh Dickenson, 2005).